LONG ROAD SOUTH:
THE PAN AMERICAN HIGHWAY

This edition belongs to...

LONG ROAD SOUTH

The Pan American Highway

LONG ROAD
The Pan American Highway

BY JOSEPH R. YOGERST
PHOTOGRAPHS BY SUSIE POST AND MELISSA FARLOW

NATIONAL
GEOGRAPHIC

WASHINGTON, D.C.

SOUTH

UNITED STATES

Gulf of Mexico

MEXICO

Chapter 1

GUATEMALA   BELIZE

HONDURAS   Caribbean Sea

EL SALVADOR   NICARAGUA

COSTA RICA

Chapter 2   PANAMA

VENEZUELA   FRENCH GUIANA (France)

GUYANA   SURINAM

COLOMBIA

Chapter 3

ECUADOR

PACIFIC

OCEAN

PERU   BRAZIL

BOLIVIA

Chapter 4

CHILE   PARAGUAY

URUGUAY

ARGENTINA

Chapter 5

———— Pan American Highway
       covered in book

·········· Rest of Pan American
       Highway system

0   Miles   1,000
0   Kilometers   1,500

PRECEDING PAGES: *Pan American Highway along Peru's arid coast*   Melissa Farlow

CONTENTS

Veining the whole of South America, the vast Pan American Highway system now seeps across both North and South America, from Alaska to the tip of Argentina. Conceived in the climate of internationalism that followed World War I, the original 10,000-mile highway (shown in red) revolutionized life along its path. Today this ribbon of asphalt leads from the steamy Rio Grande Valley in the north to the chilly shores of Patagonia in the south, offering an intimate glimpse into the heart and soul of Latin America.

Library of Congress CIP Data appears on page 200

MEXICO

PHOTOGRAPHS BY MELISSA FARLOW

It seemed more a marketplace than a political margin, a river of humanity that swirled all around me as I left Laredo, Texas, crossing the muddy Rio Grande on International Bridge Number One into Mexico. Hundreds of other people were crossing the span in both directions, hauling boxes and bags, dickering with the vendors and the money changers working the middle of the bridge. A cop blew his whistle to keep everyone moving, but it was no use. People were too caught up in the spirit of buying and selling to worry about things like traffic flow and international protocol.

At the other end of the bridge was Nuevo Laredo, the first stop in a countless string of cities and towns that would take me all the way through Latin America to the southern tip of Argentina. This was no arbitrary journey. I had a specific plan, a definite objective: Tracing the roughly 10,000-mile path of the original Pan American Highway, a journey that would take the better part of three months.

In the history of humankind no one has ever attempted to build a single roadway across such a vast distance, through so many different climatic, vegetation, and geologic zones. The idea for the highway took root in 1923 when the Fifth International Conference of American States created a Pan American Highway Commission to help plan and distribute funds for the project. It was at the brink of an era of engineering superlatives—Hoover Dam, the Golden Gate Bridge, the Empire State Building—and no one batted an eye at the construction of a road that would stretch through a dozen nations. Although each of the countries along the route agreed to contribute funds to the project, the United States accepted most of the initial burden, viewing the highway as a pathway to international solidarity, commerce, and communication. Construction began around 1930 and was nearly finished by the outbreak of World War II. In the decades since, countless spur roads and alternative routes have been added to the Pan American Highway system, tentacles of asphalt that spread across Latin American like a giant octopus. And now the highway extends north all the way to Alaska.

PEDESTRIANS DASH THROUGH *an underground walkway that leads onto International Bridge Number One, oldest existing link between Mexico's Nuevo Laredo and Laredo, Texas. More than four million people—commuters, shoppers, and sightseers—walk across the bridge each year.*

PRECEDING PAGES: *Texans "Shorty" Vaught and his son Jason get into the rhythm of a* norteño *band in a Nuevo Laredo cantina. Americans flock to the quirky border town for nightlife, pharmaceuticals, even inexpensive dentistry.*

EVEN IN EARLY MORNING International Bridge Number Two, downstream from Laredo, Texas, on the Rio Grande, clogs with trucks heading from Mexico into the United States. Since the 1992 signing of the North American Free Trade Agreement, truck traffic on the three international bridges has increased 100 percent.

Opposite: Monterrey flaunts its flair for the cosmopolitan during Expo Tu Boda, a bridal fashion show at the city's convention center. With more than three million people, Monterrey is the country's third largest city, an economic power-house with close ties to the U.S.

Faro del comercio—Lighthouse of Commerce—looms above Monterrey's baroque cathedral. Mexico's tallest monument, the 230-foot concrete sculpture symbolizes urban renewal; a laser light at its top sweeps the city by night.

Some measure of the original highway's success can be gleaned from the annals of early trips along the route. In 1928 three Brazilians set off on a road journey to the U.S. It took them nine years to reach Washington, D.C. In 1941, when most of the highway was finished, four Argentines completed a similar trip in just seven months. Today you could probably drive the Latin American portion of the highway in less than two weeks. But I wasn't trying to set any records. My goal was to get to know the highway, the landscapes, and peoples along its rambling path.

International Bridge Number One empties onto Nuevo Laredo's Avenida Guerrero, a block-long strip of liquor stores, pharmacies, and root canal specialists that marks the very first mile of the original Pan American. As I crawled along in midday traffic, a young man jogged beside my car. "You want parking?" he shouted. "You want dentist?" When none of that worked, he tried a little border humor. "Maybe diet pills?" he said with a sly smile. But that was as hard as the sell got. Despite its frontline position on a frontier cursed by crime, smuggling, and ethnic tension, Nuevo Laredo was nothing like the hard-boiled border towns I knew from farther west. With over 400,000 people, it's more than twice the size of its American sister, Laredo. But the cities boast a similar southwestern ambience, crowded with shops and bars, the monotony of one-story buildings broken occasionally by a church spire or modest high-rise. Both populations are largely Hispanic, and even in Laredo Spanish is heard more than English. If not for Old Glory and the Mexican Tricolor fluttering on either side of the Rio Grande, it would be hard to tell the two cities apart.

South of Nuevo Laredo, the Pan American Highway shoots across the scrubland of northern Mexico, a vast expanse of cactus, sagebrush, and mesquite trees interrupted by the occasional ranch house. Most people driving along the smooth, four-lane road probably see nothing more than a big empty space. But as I scanned the desolate terrain, more than a hundred years of history unfolded in my mind. Gen. Antonio López de Santa Anna marched through this region in 1836 on his way to a face-off with Davy Crockett and Jim Bowie at the Alamo. During the American Civil War, Confederates stockpiled cotton here, then shippped it out to avoid Union blockades; during Prohibition, it was a haven for bootleggers. Through most of the Mexican Revolution (1910-1920), it was the realm of Francisco "Pancho" Villa, the notorious bandit and guerilla leader who was chased by the *federales* and then by Gen. John Pershing. When Villa began raiding U.S. border towns, Pershing's cavalry stalked him back and forth across northern Mexico for nearly a year but never caught him. In the end, the flamboyant guerilla was gunned down by Mexican assassins.

One of Villa's hideouts was Monterrey, nestled at the base of the Sierra Madre Oriental and the first city of any size on the southward journey from the border. Villa would hardly recognize the place today. Once sleepy Monterrey has grown in recent years into the economic superstar of Mexico. An industrial giant and financial center with three million people, it likes to call itself Sultana del Norte—Sultan of the North. With good reason. The city claims more university students, more computers, and a higher literacy rate than any other Mexican metropolis.

Monterrey's most celebrated factory is Cervecería Cuauhtémoc, which spans both sides of the highway on the northern outskirts of downtown. Founded in 1890, the brewery produces millions of bottles of Carta Blanca, Bohemia, and Tecate beer each day. The oldest building, a lovely brick structure smothered in ivy, has been converted into one the country's premier modern art museums. Perched among the old copper brewing vats are masterpieces by muralist Diego Rivera and his most celebrated wife (he had several), Frida Kahlo.

Another part of the complex houses a baseball museum, the entrance guarded by statues of Babe Ruth and Fernando Valenzuela. I learned inside that Mexico's love affair with baseball stretches back to pre-Columbian days—ball games played by ancient Olmec, Maya, and Aztec peoples. There were other exhibits on the Mexican professional league and the multitude of Mexican players that have hit and pitched their way into the American major leagues. Before leaving, I took my turn in the indoor batting cage, whacking a couple of fast balls out of my imaginary park.

My first detour off the main highway was west to Cumbres de Monterrey National Park, one of Mexico's largest nature preserves. Heavily wooded and rugged, the park encompasses nearly 1,000 square miles of the Sierra Madre Oriental, including the handsome Cascada Cola de Caballo (Horsetail Fall), which tumbles 75 feet over a natural limestone shelf near Villa de Santiago. To reach the fall, I had to walk about a mile upstream through an oak-laden canyon. The area was bathed in an early morning calm broken only by the sound of rushing water and birds rustling through the underbrush. Autumn was in the air, a hint of color on the leaves and a slight chill in the breeze blowing down from the Sierra. On the edge of the fall I found a small hut, an elderly man mending its wooden gate. He smiled and introduced himself as José "Nacho" Rocha, a photographer who has made his living at the fall for 50 years, snapping shots of people who forgot to bring their own cameras.

"I've been up here every day, seven days a week, since I was a boy," Nacho bragged in broken English. Producing a battered old Polaroid, he offered to snap my picture. Besides being a businessman, Nacho seemed to know all there was to know about Horsetail Fall and the preserve. He reeled off tales about the park's limestone caverns, petroglyphs, and wildlife. "This place is especially beautiful in winter," Nacho declared. "Sometimes there is snow on the mountains behind the fall. So nice!"

Leaving Nacho, I followed one of the highway's oldest sections, a strip along the eastern flank of the Sierra Madre that dates from 1936. Despite its age, the road was in good repair with few of the gaping holes or asphalt ripples that would become routine in southern Mexico. I had a mighty distance to cover that day—more than 300 miles—but it was one of the most diverse stretches I would encounter along the entire route. The countless orange groves around Linares have made it Mexico's "citrus bowl" in recent years, and beyond the groves lanky longhorn cattle grazed endless ranchlands. South of Ciudad Victoria, the highway crept into verdant mesa country and crossed the Tropic of Cancer, marked by a cement globe and a small café with goats grazing outside. Plunging into the tropical lowlands of the Río Tamesi Valley, the terrain changed dramatically to jungle and sugarcane fields—although the most astonishing sight was a huge tarantula scampering across the roadway. It was after dark by the time I rolled into Ciudad Valles, the last few miles lit by fireflies dancing through the roadside brush.

Beyond Ciudad Valles is "Indian country"—the heartland of the Huastec civilization that has flourished in this region for at least 6,000 years. The Huastec aren't nearly as well known as the Aztec or Toltec, but among the great tribes of central Mexico theirs is the only one that has survived into the 20th century. About 90,000 Huastec reside in the rugged hills south of Ciudad Valles, most of them oblivious to modern life, many still living in thatch-roofed homes. On Sunday mornings, a great open-air market unfolds in the streets and plaza of Tancanhuitz, one of the largest Huastec centers in the region. Most of the vendors are Indian women in traditional *quechquémal* tunics, their raven braids brightened with strands of colored wool. They sell sugarcane, avocados, pork tamales, beeswax candles, gourd containers, woven shoulder bags, and clumps of black copal, an incense that comes from a tree of the same name.

In an alley beside the market, Huastec farmers were selling piglets corralled in makeshift wooden pens. One young farmer hurled corn into their midst and the little porkers scrambled to eat, showing potential buyers how active and strong they were. A husband and wife seemed interested but rather hesitant about which animal they should choose. The farmer fetched a black pig by its hind feet, held it aloft. "This one is *muy macho*," he proclaimed in Spanish. But they didn't look impressed. They wanted something cheaper. The farmer grabbed another pig. Furious negotiations ensued. Finally, the couple agreed on a pig and a price: 150 pesos (roughly $15) for a pink piglet. The farmer tied a lariat around the animal's neck, and the couple led him away.

In the midst of this Huastec world, I stumbled onto something positively 20th century: a sprawling villa called Las Pozas tucked among the jungle-shrouded hills near Xilitla. The house and gardens were the byproducts of one man's fertile imagination. English surrealist artist Sir Edward James (a grandson of King Edward VII) passed through Xilitla in 1945 during a lengthy exploration of Mexico. For some time the eccentric artist had been searching for a retreat from the rigors of the modern world,

MEXICAN ARMY PATROLS *a stretch of the Pan American Highway that winds through Los Mármoles National Park in Hidalgo state. Tucked in the rugged Sierra Madre Oriental south of Tamazunchale, the park is renowned for its sheer marble cliffs and thick pine forest.*

FOLLOWING PAGES: *Cascada Cola de Caballo—Horsetail Fall—makes a dramatic 75-foot drop through Cumbres de Monterrey. Mexico's largest wilderness preserve, it protects red-rock canyons, petroglyphs, caverns, and abundant wildlife.*

a place to render his art in harmony with nature. This is where he found it.

I spent a couple of hours wandering the grounds, an isolated paradise at once exhilarating and lonely. A friend of Dalí, Picasso, and Magritte among others, he had both the time and money to complete his dream house: A labyrinth of giant concrete columns, arches, windows, and walls encased in vines, branches, and roots—a surreal Angkor Wat nestled in the Sierra Madre. James lived among the Huastec, adding to his whimsical retreat, until his death in 1984. Las Pozas is now managed by a private foundation and open to the public.

Beyond the Huastec region, the Pan American Highway crawls into Hidalgo state through a rugged knot of mountains that marks the sharp divide between the steamy Gulf lowlands and the high basins that dominate central Mexico. I found it tough going, not just the twisting road—and the thousand-foot cliffs—but also thick fog that dropped visibility to less than a car length. The road cut across Los Mármoles National Park, famed for its marble cliffs and thick pine forests, then dropped into the semidesert barrens around Zimapán. The sun broke out but not for long.

When I reached southern Hidalgo, dark clouds were rolling in and rain drops splattered the windshield. Near Pachuca, the old road finally merged with the new super-highway arrowing into the Valley of Mexico, which hovers 7,300 feet above sea level. For the first time all day I felt myself relax, knowing that one of the most treacherous mountain sections of the Pan American was finally behind me.

By the time I got off the road for the night, I was about 30 miles north of Mexico City, in its sprawling outskirts. In the morning, I woke early and went out for a walk through dawn light that hinted at a glorious sunrise to come. By daybreak I was standing at the southern end of the Avenue of the Dead, a ceremonial "street" that bisects the ancient city of Teotihuacan. As the first rays of sun hit the mountain behind, a radiant curtain slowly fell across the ruins. The ancient Mesoamerican creation myth was unfolding before my eyes. Rebirth with each sunrise—a spectacle of stone, light, and shadow that still impresses.

Later in the day I explored Teotihuacan at some length. The primary building material is *tezontle*, a lightweight volcanic stone. The pyramids' "step" design features a single stairway ascending to a flat plateau. But the surrounding palaces boast ornate decoration, including striking images of jaguars, butterflies, snakes, and birds. Not much is known about the city's original builders. They disappeared without a trace around A.D. 700, leaving no record of their origin, history, or fate. The Aztec arrived on the scene about A.D. 1200. Awed by the site's intrinsic majesty, they synthesized the ancient remains with their own religion, transforming Teotihuacan into the sacred heart of Aztec culture, the place where the sun, the moon, and humankind were born, as well as the place where humans would ascend to become gods. *(Continued on page 28)*

ON THE EDGE OF THE PAN AMERICAN HIGHWAY, *the front yard of a Huastec Indian family serves as the setting for soccer, clothes drying, and communal gatherings. Despite the soccer show, most Huastec still follow the old ways, living in thatched adobe houses and surviving on farming.*

HUASTEC FARMER *José Ramirez dickers with a local housewife over the price of a young pig at the weekly Sunday market in the town of Tancanhuitz.*

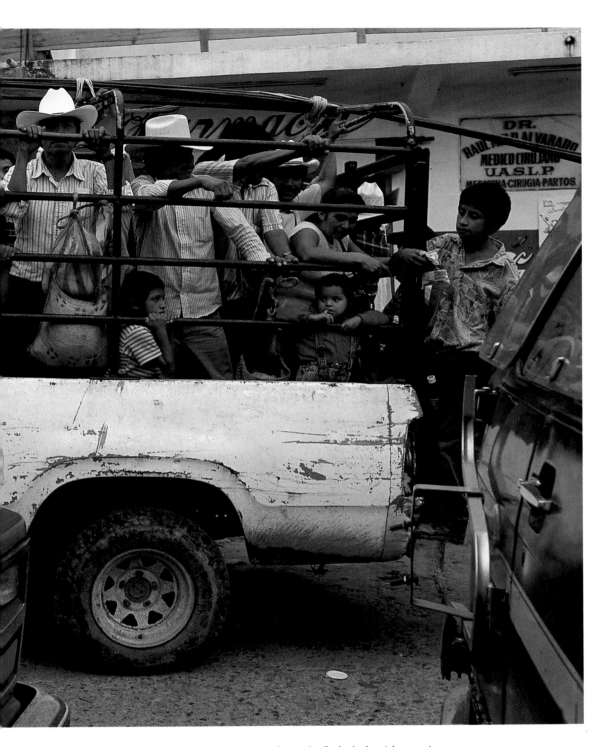

HOMEWARD-BOUND FARM FAMILIES *crowd into the flatbed of a pickup taxi , as the open-air market in Xilitla draws to an end. One of the largest Huastec towns, Xilitla and its narrow cobbled streets are filled with the stalls selling locally grown coffee and sugarcane, copal incense, and huge corn tamales.*

DINERS AT THE GRAN HOTEL'S *rooftop restaurant enjoy a bird's-eye view of the zócalo, Mexico City's grandiose main square. Built atop ruins of the ancient Aztec city of Tenochtitlán, the zócalo is now surrounded by such sprawling Spanish colonial behemoths as the Metropolitan Cathedral. In the Plaza Garibaldi (below right) mariachis gather for their nightly serenading, catering to crowds of both gringos and Mexicans.*

FOLLOWING PAGES: *Mexican schoolchildren snake through the ruins of Teotihuacan, on the northern outskirts of modern Mexico City. During its 2,000-year history, the ancient city has been venerated as a sacred sight by many cultures, including the Aztec, their predecessors, and modern-day lovers of antiquities.*

EVERY GUIDEBOOK I HAD CONSULTED, every person I had spoken with, had warned of the hazards of driving in Mexico City—insufferable traffic, belligerent motorists, an abundance of one-way streets, and very little parking. With that in mind, I decided to leave my rental car in Teotihuacan and take a taxi into town. An hour later, after wading through horrendous traffic, the taxi discharged me in front of an old colonial hotel overlooking the Alameda, a leafy park in the heart of the capital.

It's difficult to come to terms with any city but especially one that boasts 18 million inhabitants spread across 580 square miles. Residents deal with these onerous dimensions by breaking everything down into smaller levels. Their neighborhood becomes their village, an oasis of intimacy in the urban desert; many residents rarely venture into other parts of the city except on special occasions or weekend outings. That seemed like an ideal way for me to confront the world's second largest city. After a few days, the area around the Alameda started to feel snug and familiar, my own village in the heart of the Mexican capital.

One of the things I learned about this area is that old traditions die hard. Mariachis still gather each night in Plaza Garibaldi to play songs to passersby and strum among themselves. Young lovers still monopolize park benches in the Alameda, staring into one another's eyes or locked in never-ending kisses. Older couples still twirl away the afternoon at the Salon Los Angeles and other traditional dance halls. Ladies in fur coats still jostle for seats at Sanborn's, not so much a coffee shop as a shrine to 16th-century colonial architecture with murals, wrought-iron chandeliers, and carved wooden ceilings. Without fail, a military color guard still assembles in the *zócalo,* the square, at dusk to lower the Mexican flag.

Another bulwark of this neighborhood is the world-famous Ballet Folklórico, which performs at the Palacio de Bellas Artes twice a week. A showcase for music and dance traditions from throughout Mexico, the ballet is one of the country's primary reserves of local artistry. At the troupe's headquarters near Plaza Garibaldi, I talked with Viviana Basanta, the artistic director and prima ballerina, about the enduring importance of tradition in Mexican culture. "Sometimes outside influence is so strong that it starts to take over," Viviana admitted. "I think some music and dances have already been lost. But I'm happy to say that all over Mexico I find young people who want to carry on these traditions."

That night I saw Viviana dance at Bellas Artes. The show featured everything from a polka-inspired number introduced by immigrants from Eastern Europe to an atavistic deer dance created by Indian tribes in the Sonoran Desert. The audience had its fair share of tourists, but the majority were Mexicans, including many teenagers riveted by the performances.

The following morning I woke to a different sort of local tradition: the annual feast day at San Judas Tadeo Church near the Alameda. The festivities kicked off with a fireworks barrage at the crack of dawn. By sunrise thousands of people were gathered outside the shrine, many clad in green-sashed Roman-style togas, like that of their patron saint.

"We've got things going on all day," said a man selling silver *milagros* (amulets) and holy cards. And not just spiritual events. It was like a country carnival come to the big city—rides, games, music, and dozens of food stalls with culinary delights from all around Mexico. Green tortillas filled with meat, a warm drink made from corn and goat milk, sugary sweet *buñuelos* (cinnamon pastries), and deep-fried pork. The vendor at a pork stall promoted his fare as a miracle food. "This meat is so powerful, anyone who eats it will be able to speak English," he told me. He didn't miss a beat when I pointed out that I was already a native English speaker. "Then you will be able to speak perfect Spanish. Here, try it!"

Among all this fanfare, I found people waiting in line to venerate one of Mexico's newest religious icons: the Virgin of the Metro, a piece of subway pavement enshrined within glass in front of San Judas. Devotees swear they can see a likeness of the Virgin Mary in the concrete and stone. The image was discovered in 1997 after water damaged the flooring in the Hidalgo Metro Station. Thousands of people crowded into the subway to worship the Virgin, causing angry outbursts between the faithful and frustrated commuters. Municipal authorities wisely resolved to move the sacred stone to the surface, where it no longer poses a public-safety risk.

I slipped past the pavement pilgrims and into the Metro, riding a train to Coyoacán on the southern fringe of the capital. Even more than Mexico City's other districts, this area retains its village atmosphere. Built by the Spanish more than 450 years ago, Coyoacán is now the haunt of artists, writers, intellectuals, and free spirits, who have turned its leafy plazas and narrow streets into a south-of-the-border version of Greenwich Village. Coyoacán has always been a place of misfits and mavericks. It was here that conquistador Hernán Cortés built a house for Malinche, the Indian maiden who became his advisor and mistress. Considered a traitor by many Mexicans, her turncoat legacy is reflected in the term *malinchismo,* which denotes someone enamored with foreign lovers or objects.

Frida Kahlo also lived in Coyoacán, and in nearby San Angel with Diego Rivera. Here the two could indulge in their political intrigues and romantic liaisons—and sometimes their art—away from the prying eyes of the Mexican establishment. Rivera and Kahlo, among the country's foremost painters, had a turbulent marriage that endured several illicit affairs and Kahlo's frequent bouts of depression and self-loathing, themes that are obvious in her artwork. Kahlo's house has become a place of pilgrimage for feminists from worldwide. The sprawling colonial villa, painted a dazzling navy blue, is set around a courtyard filled with pre-Columbian artifacts and tropical plants. Inside are dozens of Kahlo's paintings, and mementos of her turbulent life—including a four-poster bed mounted with a large mirror so that Frida could stare at her own image.

COMBINATION COFFEEHOUSE AND BOOKSTORE, *Puebla's Teorema attracts a young crowd with its poetry readings and folk music. One of Mexico's most cultured cities, Puebla overflows with art galleries, craft shops, and museums.*

Another celebrated Coyoacán resident was Russian revolutionary Leon Trotsky. He took refuge here in 1937 after a confrontation with Stalin led to his expulsion from the Soviet Union. "Trotsky was always worried about being attacked and killed," guide Jesus Vargas explained as we strolled through the lush tropical gardens around the one-story, stucco mansion. "He built brick guard towers in each corner of the compound and steel gates at the entrance. But there were so many Stalinist spies around. They were everywhere in Mexico City!"

The first attempt on Trotsky's life was launched by Stalinist agents armed with tommy guns. "Here you can still see the bullet holes," Jesus pointed out, sweeping his hand across the wall above Trotsky's bed. The second attempt—a lone assassin with an ice axe—succeeded. Not much has changed since that day in 1940. Trotsky's wire-rim glasses lie on the desk in the study where the assassin struck him down. His suits hang in the nearby closet, his toothbrush poised above the bathroom sink. I found it all rather eerie. But Mexicans have never shied away from death.

RETRIEVING THE CAR FROM TEOTIHUACAN, I made my way around rather than through Mexico City, but the various ring roads and bypasses were choked with trucks and buses trying the same ploy. I was halfway to Puebla before the vast metropolis faded into farmland and pine forest. I caught a glimpse of white out of the corner of my eye and looked up at two massive volcanoes—17,887-foot Popocatépetl and 17,343-foot Ixtaccíhuatl—hovering above the highway, another sign that I was finally leaving the crowded Valley of Mexico.

Forsaking the modern toll road, I followed the old route of the Pan American Highway around the eastern base of the mountains. In anticipation of the impending Day of the Dead celebration, trucks laden with gold and scarlet flowers were rumbling in the opposite direction, headed for markets in Mexico City. Along the roadside, families and friends of accident victims were arranging floral wreaths and other tributes. It was a touching scene, and also sobering—what a vast number of people had perished on this relatively short stretch of highway.

Soon the volcanoes came into sharp view again, the elongated body of Ixtaccíhuatl and the smoking cinder-cone pyramid of Popocatépetl, ever present reminders that Mother Nature still rules in this part of Mexico. People in this region have literally lived in the shadow of the volcanoes since prehistoric times, and not long after my visit "Popo" exploded with a series of violent eruptions that shattered windows, roof tiles, and brick walls. "It's a monster, but a very precious monster because it also gives us life by enriching the soil," said agronomist Rene Aboilar. "People in the little pueblos near the volcano know it is very dangerous. But they are *muy campechana* (very laid back). They are accustomed to the smoke and steam and tremors. It's a very curious thing, but the farmers don't have fear."

Snow-crowned Popocatépetl backdrops a field of flowers near Atlixco, in the Puebla Valley. The golden zempazuchitl *blooms decorate graveyards and churches all over Mexico during the October Day of the Dead festival.*

Following pages: Family members mount all-night, Day of the Dead vigil over the grave of a loved one in the municipal cemetery at Xoxocotlán. Candles, incense, fresh flowers, and three-dimensional sand paintings turn burial sites into festive settings, as revelers eat, drink, and sing to show their disdain for death.

My favorite town along this stretch of highway was Huejotzingo, famed for its "cider champagne"; huge bottles of peaches marinated in it were sold along the main street. The town is also famous for its 16th-century Franciscan convent, among the oldest missions in Mexico. Mauricio Alfaro, a young seminarian from Puebla, was dusting off ancient statues in the church when I entered. He happily answered my questions.

"The history of Huejotzingo is very grand," he beamed, explaining that the area had been home to the Nahua Indians when Cortés marched this way in 1519. Already subjugated by the Aztecs, the Nahua gladly aided the Spanish in their quest. Franciscan padres traveling with Cortés erected a mission church at Huejotzingo. "The Franciscans typically built where the agriculture was rich," Mauricio explained, "and they recognized this area was fertile because of the volcanic soil." Huejotzingo quickly became a center for the Roman Catholic evangelization of Mexico. The padres built a grand plaza outside the church, a marketplace where local Indians exchanged goods and were exposed to Catholic beliefs. "The pagans, or unconverted, had to stay in the plaza. They weren't allowed inside where the ceremonies and processions took place. You couldn't join the fiesta unless you converted, so most of the Indians became Christians."

Another 30 minutes down the highway stood Puebla, a bastion of baroque churches and colonial mansions that glistened in the noonday sun. People moved at such a languid pace it hardly seemed the country's fourth largest metropolis. Puebla's trademark is the Talavera tile—hand-painted, terra-cotta squares named after the Spanish city where the style originated. Manufactured in local workshops, Puebla flaunts its Talavera just about everywhere: wrapped around fountains, smothering church domes, covering entire structures in the downtown area. The city also is renowned for its mole, a thick, spicy sauce that has become a culinary hallmark of southern Mexico. At Fonda Santa Clara, a typical local restaurant, the waiter swore that their mole recipe was exactly the same as that devised by the nuns of Santa Rosa Convent more than 400 years ago. Whether or not the sauce was the authentic baroque mixture, the meal was divine— a combination of green chili, red chili, and dark brown chocolate mole over chicken enchiladas.

Walking off the meal, I wandered up to the Jardín de los Trabajos, where the city's mariachis gather each evening. Clad in black sombreros and tight black suits with silver studs, the musicians are as much a part of Puebla as the city's famous tiles. One mariachi stood out from the rest, a large man in a metallic blue suit. "I'm a singer," he said, explaining his attire. "We are allowed to be more flamboyant." His name was José Perez, a mariachi crooner for more than 20 years. "This is the only thing I really wanted to do with my life," José declared. "When I was young, I learned by listening to records, listening to other mariachis." I asked José to name his favorite songs. He smiled and said *(Continued on page 42)*

(Continued on page 42)

HIS BURROS LADEN WITH FIREWOOD, *a farmer heads to a mescal factory in rural Oaxaca, where 80 percent of Mexico's mescal is produced. The potent liquor is made by roasting the heart of wild agave—century plant—in ovens, then milling, fermenting, and distilling it.*

FOLLOWING PAGES: *Grandmother Isidra Carballido and her six-year-old granddaughter Cecilia Mateos search a Oaxaca cornfield for grasshoppers; fried, the insects make a tasty dinner dish.*

ON HER 15TH BIRTHDAY, *an Indian girl (opposite) in Juchitán attends communion at the Catholic church. Despite the Catholic overlay, Zapotec culture remains strong here in the Isthmus of Tehuantepec. Never part of the Aztec world and resistant to the Spanish, the Zapotec continue their independent ways to this day.*

TWO WOMEN TRIP THE LIGHT FANTASTIC *at a wedding party in Juchitán. Off the dance floor, Zapotec women often take the lead in business and government.*

"Whatever people ask for." But love songs were his specialty. "If a man wants to ask a woman to marry him, he can hire me to sing a song of proposal." He broke into an impromptu melody that drifted into the starry night.

I was on the road again the following morning, driving through some of the loveliest scenery I would see in all of Mexico. South of Puebla, the Pan American passed endless flower fields, golden *zempazuchitl* and scarlet *terciopelo* being harvested for the Day of the Dead. Soon the floral bounty gave way to a wilderness of candelabra and cardon cactus that spread as far as the eye could see. Other than the occasional burro munching wildflowers at the side of the road, there were few signs of human habitation, a welcome contrast to the milling throngs of urban Mexico. Vistas of deep valleys and interminable mountains were shaded purple in the late afternoon light, and every so often I caught a fleeting glimpse of 18,855-foot Pico de Orizaba, the volcano that is Mexico's highest peak.

But something cruel happened as I crossed into Oaxaca state. The highway deteriorated into potholes, and the wilderness faded into a wasteland of erosion. The land was beyond redemption, spent by centuries of overgrazing and deforestation so extreme it looked as if it had been strip-mined. This went on for hours, mile after mile of ravaged earth, a glaring illustration of why so many rural Oaxacans have migrated to the big cities and border regions in search of a better life. "This is a very old land and maybe a little tired," one villager told me. "Each year it gets a little worse. There are not many things to do here, not many jobs. That is why so many of the *campesinos* (farmers) leave."

Yet amid this devastation I found a shred of redemption. In dusty Yanhuitlan, a baroque church called Santo Domingo de Guzman looms above the Pan American. Built in the late 1500s by Dominican friars, the interior is embellished with incredible wooden statues modeled with classic Spanish iconography. Human-hair wigs and handmade clothing make them so lifelike, you feel you could be staring into the faces of people who lived four centuries ago. Many of the wooden statues were on the brink of total decay until a restoration effort was launched in the 1960s by Mexico's National Institute of Anthropology and History. The caretaker told me that some of the funding comes from Oaxacans now living in Los Angeles, who want to give something back to the poor community from which they came. The church has been rescued, giving hope that maybe someday the surrounding countryside can also be salvaged.

It was another three hours of twists and turns before the highway finally dropped down into the broad valley that harbors Oaxaca City. There is nothing else like it in all of Mexico, a city that gracefully blends Spanish colonial and indigenous Indian touches, a place where pedestrians still take precedence over motor vehicles, a spot where artistry rather than worth is the major talking point.

Case in point: a recent major restoration of the 16th-century Santo

DEVILS, TRANSVESTITES, GUERRILLAS, *anything goes as costumed Day of the Dead revelers march down the Pan American Highway in San Pedro Totolapán. Parade participants stop traffic to solicit handouts from drivers; if no pesos appear, the driver is generally treated to verbal abuse.*

IN TROUBLED CHIAPAS, soldiers chat with a Maya mother. Since 1994 periodic conflict has erupted between the army and local Zapatista rebels demanding more assistance from the federal government.

OPPOSITE: Intent on listening to her teacher, a Chiapas first grader stands on her chair to gain a little height in a classroom of mixed ages. The 120 students in this village school learn in Spanish and their native Maya. Hoping to win local trust, the government has initiated programs to improve schools and health care.

Domingo Convent. Although the Monte Albán treasure room, with its priceless gold, silver, and turquoise trinkets, is the museum's most popular exhibit, there is literally something for everyone…even for a writer traveling the Pan American. In one of the rooms on the upper floor I found a space devoted to the highway's legacy. Altimeters, compasses, and metal tape measures used during the road's original construction were displayed, and an old newsreel extolled the highway's virtues: It permitted better connections between isolated communities; accelerated the introduction of technological changes like electricity; spurred a resurgence in industries like fishing and coffee cultivation; improved access to archaeological sites; and greatly increased tourist activity. In other words, Oaxaca state would not be what it is today if not for the Pan American.

Bewitched by Santo Domingo, I almost forgot that the city's most important holiday was unfolding outside. A nationwide celebration, the Day of the Dead (Día de los Muertos) serves as an homage to late friends and relatives and gives the living an opportunity to show their machismo by laughing in the face of death. Although largely based on the Catholic All Saints' Day, the ritual also draws inspiration from an ancient Aztec festival that used human sacrifices to ensure the rebirth of deceased kinfolk. These days, there's a touch of gringo Halloween—Mexican kids dressed like witches, vampires, and goblins—thrown in.

Death is handled cabaret style during the three-day festival, as Oaxaca—and Mexico—explode with music, dance, and food. Brass bands circle the zócalo, trailed by troupes of dancers in outrageous costumes. Housewives compete to make the best *pulque* (cactus moonshine) and *pan de muerto* (breads with skulls or crossbones on the crust). People break into witty *calaveras,* songs or poems eulogizing those still living.

The festival highlight for both locals and tourists is a night in a local graveyard. Thousands of people were already polishing tombstones and arranging intricate candle displays by the time I arrived at the municipal cemetery in Xoxocotlán, a village on the southern outskirts of Oaxaca. Those tasks complete, families and friends settled into graveside meals or drifted off to the various attractions around the cemetery: food stalls with great open fires, firecracker vendors, women selling wax skulls and other ghoulish artifacts. And music. Lots of music. Teenagers with boom boxes. Troubadours with guitars. Elderly women chanting religious tunes.

Well after midnight, I came upon a family gathered around a well-tended grave. The parents sat on low wooden seats, the children curled beneath blankets. One of the men was strumming ranchero tunes on his guitar and singing in a low, lovely voice. The family saw me watching, and, not wanting me to feel left out, dispatched one of the children with homemade tamales and a shot of mescal tequila. A simple act of hospitality, but it spoke volumes about the brotherhood and compassion that infuses life in Mexico.

REPAIR WORK ON THE PAN AMERICAN near Escopetazo slows traffic in the Chiapas highlands. The highway through southern Mexico and much of Central America was heavily damaged in 1998, as Hurricane Mitch swept the region, washing away pavement and bridges; heavy flooding in 1999 created more havoc.

CENTRAL AMERICA

PHOTOGRAPHS BY SUSIE POST

I hadn't gone a hundred miles in Guatemala before traffic on the Pan American came to a complete stop. The source of the bottleneck was a band of Maya wielding protest banners and wooden planks full of nails, which they had dragged across a busy junction near Quezaltenango. The local cops looked on with mild amusement. They had seen this sort of thing before, just eight days before during an earlier demonstration. A couple of UN observers, making sure that nobody's human rights were violated, looked equally blasé, slouched deep into their air-conditioned pickup. The only people who seemed the least bit fazed were disgruntled motorists, some of whom had been delayed by the Maya barricade for more than three hours.

I tracked down one of the protest leaders, a young Maya named Aroldo Perez. Clad in baseball cap, white sneakers, and denim jacket, eyes hidden behind aviator shades, he was the very picture of a trendy militant. "This is one way we can put pressure on the government," Aroldo explained. "We are trying to make them aware that the reforms promised in the peace accord of 1996 have not been met. The government has made these laws on paper but not in practice. We also want the public to know that we have these rights." It didn't seem to matter to Aroldo and his companions that the government ministers and legislators who could actually respond to Maya demands—like land reform and official recognition of indigenous languages—were more than a hundred miles away in Guatemala City. "The wind takes our words," Aroldo said confidently.

The Maya protest was a portent of things to come, a string of natural and man-made obstructions that would make Central America the most troublesome portion of my journey along the Pan American Highway. Potholes and pesky fellow drivers plagued the roads through this region. But they were the least of my worries. I also had to contend with striking truck drivers, odious border officials, and the destruction caused by Hurricane Mitch just a couple of months before my passage. At the end of all this calamity was the Darién Gap, where the Pan American peters out, becoming a muddy jungle track.

MARKET DAY in San Juan Atitán becomes a showcase of Maya colors and styles, as local farmers sport traditional dress…and the younger ones their Walkman-style headsets. Western Guatemala's highlands remain a hotbed of indigenous culture, where ancient ways persist, despite an occasional bow to technology.

PRECEDING PAGES: Eerie blue light shrouds Lago de Atitlán in the still before dawn. Rugged mountain terrain and Maya villages ring Guatemala's most renowned lake, now a popular retreat for gringo backpackers and retirees.

In the Guatemala highlands near Zunil, Francisco Estacuy works his milpa—mountainside cornfield. Despite rich volcanic soil, many of the region's farmers eke out only a meager existence; the poverty has ignited a long, bloody civil war between guerrilla groups and the central government.

FOLLOWING PAGES: *Recess erupts at the Escuela Nacional Urbana Mixta in Todos Santos, one of western Guatemala's most solidly Maya towns. Though education has improved slightly in recent years, 55 percent of Guatemala's citizens receive no schooling at all, leaving 45 percent of the population illiterate.*

I had a very difficult three weeks ahead of me. But I wouldn't face the hurdles alone. Relinquishing the rental car that had taken me across Mexico, I hired a driver to spirit me most of the way across Central America in a 4x4 pickup. I found Mariano Boj through a friend who had taken a Spanish language course in Quezaltenango, Mariano's hometown. A retired brewery worker and labor union organizer, Mariano was more than just a solid driver. He was also a homespun philosopher who had an opinion on almost everything we encountered along the highway. A most worthy travel companion.

A day after linking up, Mariano and I drove into the Sierra Cuchumatanes of western Guatemala, to a secluded village called Todos Santos. Here, as in much of the traditional Maya stronghold that extends across eastern Mexico into Guatemala, ancient ways and means persist on the cusp of the 21st century. The town is governed by an indigenous council, and the Maya calendar is still sometimes observed. But the most conspicuous cultural statement is the local attire.

Unlike other parts of Central America, where T-shirts and jeans are now standard garb, the Maya haven't cast off their traditional clothes. The women of Todos Santos wear dark blue skirts and blood red blouses; the men sport red pants with white stripes, black chaps, and towering cowboy hats. It's a hackneyed phrase, but time really has stood still when it comes to Todos Santos fashion. "The people of Todos Santos have been able to keep their traditional dress, language, and customs because of our very impassioned pride," said local teacher Benito Ramirez, clad in his own bright red pants. "We try to emphasize this to our children."

Along the muddy main street of Todos Santos I noticed a small mud-brick structure shaped like a Hershey's chocolate kiss. Gray-haired Amelia Mendoza was weaving on the nearby patio, and I asked her what she baked in such a large oven. "No, no, no. It's not an oven," she laughed. "It's a Maya sweat house. That's how we bathe ourselves." You have to crawl into the homemade sauna on your hands and knees. But once inside it's quite cozy, heated by burning wood and big enough for three or four adults. "You find these only at very isolated places in the highlands," Amelia added. "Mainly in Maya communities. You sit there awhile and start to sweat and then clean yourself off with soap and water."

A couple of days later I came across more Maya traditions in Chichicastenango. The town is famous for its Spanish colonial architecture and the sprawling market that unfolds every Thursday and Sunday in the main square, drawing busloads of gringo tourists. Looming over the plaza are the twin spires of the Santo Tomás church, where ancient Maya rites blend easily with Roman Catholic tradition to create that hybrid faith unique to this part of the world.

The cloud of incense hovering in the nave was so thick I could barely see the altar. Hundreds of candles blocked my passage up the center aisle, tended by Indian women with scarves wrapped tightly round their heads. The wooden saints perched above the pews were clad in rich Maya textiles, their niches decorated with feathers, flowers, and food offerings. I watched as an elderly couple tapped candles on the feet of St. Thomas, then sprinkled his statue with holy water from a liquor bottle. They knelt in silent prayer before moving on to the next effigy.

The stone staircase in front of Santo Tomás is the realm of Maya *chuchacaos,* shamans, who gather each morning with incense and offerings. The church was erected in the 1540s on the site of an Indian shrine, and in many respects the rituals played out on the front steps harken back to the rites once performed on the massive stairways fronting Maya temples. "I'm praying for the harvest—the corn, the beans, the apples," said shaman Geronimo Pantzay as he ascended the steps, swinging a tin can with smoldering incense. "I do this every day, mostly for family members who have farms." Geronimo didn't speak English or Spanish, only a local Maya language, but it was easy to find a translator among the teenage boys hanging out in front of the church. After more than 25 years as a chuchacao, Geronimo was also empowered to perform traditional weddings and funerals, although he was quick to point out that newlyweds should hedge their bets. "When you get married, you must do both the Maya and Catholic ceremonies to make sure it's a perfect union."

Later that day I explored one of the only great Maya ruins along the Guatemala portion of the Pan American: the ancient city of Iximché, poised on a pine-studded mesa near Tecpán. The ruins aren't nearly as grand as Tikal or Chichén Itzá, but Iximché still renders a hint of Maya majesty: half a dozen stone temples and palaces in various states of repair, most of them covered in earth and grass rather than fully excavated. Founded in the late 1400s by the Kaqchikel Maya, the city flourished until 1524, when the conquistadors arrived from Mexico. For a brief time, Iximché served as the colonial capital of Spanish Central America, but it was eventually abandoned.

Mariano and I clambered up one of the larger pyramids and scouted the site; the only other visitors were a couple of young lovers smooching on the grassy carpet of an ancient ball court. Otherwise we had the ruins to ourselves. We spread our lunch across a weathered stone and tried to imagine what Iximché must have been like 500 years ago—solemn ceremonies in the temples, hustle-bustle in the markets, royal protocol in the palaces. "There's now a theory that these temples were probably used for

FOLLOWING PAGES: *Faithful illuminate the village church in Momostenango during a Sunday morning service. Beyond the quiet of the church, a boisterous weekly market is bright with handwoven ponchos and blankets, a specialty of this sheep-rearing region.*

astrological and astronomical observation," Mariano explained, munching cheese and crackers. Which is exactly what we did after lunch: determined the position of the sun and the best spot for a siesta.

By nightfall we were in Antigua Guatemala, checking into a hotel that had once been a grand colonial mansion with huge rooms set around a cobblestone courtyard. It was a preview of things to come: Antigua Guatemala has become a feast for the eyes and an exquisite example of how restoration can bring a faltering community back to life.

Founded in the 1540s, the city burgeoned into the political, economic, and cultural center of Central America. Spanish artisans and architects were commissioned to create elegant churches, plazas, and palaces. No expense was spared in transforming the capital into one of the most magnificent cities in the Americas. Its power and glory endured for just over 200 years. In July of 1773, the city was destroyed by a massive earthquake. The Spanish colonial governor mandated the construction of a new capital at Guatemala City. Antigua Guatemala was left to wither and die. It was largely lost and forgotten until the 1940s, when the picturesque ruins began to attract tourists.

It could be argued that Antigua Guatemala is now the most charming city in Central America, perhaps in all of Latin America. There are few who would disagree, especially Elizabeth Bell. An Antigua resident for more than 25 years now, the California-born historian and writer has been instrumental in Antigua's resurrection, serving for nine years with the government agency charged with preserving the city's architectural treasures. "One step out of Antigua and everything is Maya," she told me. "But inside everything is incredibly orthodox. The Spanish wanted order in the New World, so they built a Roman-Arabic-Spanish city in what was then the middle of nowhere."

I spent a morning exploring the ruins with Elizabeth, learning about restoration projects. "This is a clear example of what happens when you neglect a building for 200 years," she said as we walked through the remains of Santiago Cathedral. "This didn't all fall down at once but gradually, since 1773." Workmen were busy shoring up walls and repairing arches with a mixture of sand, lime, and dirt similar to the original 16th-century mortar. "We want to leave the cathedral as a ruin but make sure it doesn't fall down anymore," Elizabeth explained. "By the end of this year we should be able to use it again, not as a church but as an outdoor theater."

I could have spent weeks in Antigua Guatemala, but Mariano and I

SERENE AND CLASSICAL, the hot springs spa at Fuentes Georginas warms Canadian visitors Martin LeBlanc and Louanne Halle. Bubbling through the lush central highlands above Zunil, the waters draw heat from the same geothermal processes that fuel nearby volcanoes.

eventually tore ourselves away. We drove to El Salvador along a stretch of the Pan American draped in bright orange flame trees. It was the dry season, the highway was in good repair, and we made quick time to the frontier. By lunch we were creeping into San Salvador in heavy traffic, but there were plenty of things to see along the way. A traveling circus had settled along the highway, tigers pacing back and forth in their cages, the blue-and-white big top glistening in the sun. At a nearby service station, a clown in a rainbow wig tried to drum up business with salsa music and soccer-ball tricks. It was almost as if the entire city had transformed into a carnival, a joyous contrast to the days 20 years ago when San Salvador's streets flowed with the blood of civil war.

Mariano knew the border crossing between El Salvador and Honduras and predicted it would be a breeze. No such luck. The frontier at El Amatillo was blocked by a barricade of big rigs, three abreast and more than a mile long. Truckers, angry about lethargic immigration and customs procedures, had decided to shut down the border for everyone. "We're going to sleep here tonight," said one driver, crawling down from his cab. Several truckers had already strung hammocks beneath their rigs, anticipating a long strike. During the next two hours only one vehicle was allowed through the border—a pickup truck with a coffin and several dozen mourners trying to reach a funeral in El Salvador. Finally the police were called in to restore order and get traffic flowing. It was late afternoon by the time we hit asphalt again, moving through Honduran countryside recently ravaged by Hurricane Mitch.

"MALDITO TE ODIAMOS MITCH!"—"Damn You Mitch!"—read a crude hand-painted sign in Nacaome, the first town inside Honduras. The town's steel bridge, which had carried Pan American traffic for more than 50 years, had been swept away by the deluge. As we crossed the river on a makeshift causeway, I could see the bridge about a quarter mile downstream, crushed beyond repair. (I later learned that the causeway, too, was wrecked by the 1999 flooding that devastated the area.) The havoc was even more dramatic in Choluteca, where the flood zone was at least a mile wide, overturned trucks and trees scattered across the landscape. We saw this sort of destruction again and again over the next two days as we made our way across Honduras and into Nicaragua. Every valley had its own tale of woe.

It wasn't until we reached León, the old colonial city in northern Nicaragua, that a semblance of normal life was visible along the roadside. Founded in 1524, León is one of the oldest and proudest cities in Central America. For more than 400 years it has been a bastion of liberal values and one of the launch pads for the Sandinista uprising of the late 1970s. The city has a magnificent municipal cathedral, the largest church in Central America, where many notable Nicaraguans are entombed. But León's real claim to fame is its outdoor art—revolutionary murals that seem to

Backdropped by Santiago Cathedral, Antigua Guatemala's central plaza serves as a vast meeting place for local families. Founded shortly after the Spanish conquest, this colonial capital was considered the most beautiful city in the Americas until an earthquake tumbled its grandeur in 1773.

At a food stall in Chichicastenango, Maya women fry tortillas. On Thursdays and Sundays the sleepy highland town holds one of Guatemala's largest markets.

Religious procession bathes the streets of Quetzaltenango in a copal-scented swirl. For almost 400 years, the Maya here in western Guatemala have blended Catholic beliefs with traditional rituals to create their own hybrid religion.

cover almost every spare inch of wall space on facades in the city center.

Opposite the cathedral, spread across two massive walls, I found a huge mural that recounts the turbulent history of Nicaragua from the Spanish conquest through the revolution. A wasteland of bloody swords and war clubs, barbed wire and scorched battle tanks, culminating in a hopeful scene of the nation's future—children flying a kite beneath majestic volcanoes. Hovering over a nearby basketball court, a two-story painting depicts a red, white, and blue snake (the CIA) trying to strangle Nicaraguan democracy. Around another corner, I looked straight into the eyes of a massive Che Guevara. Crawling up the wall of the adjacent garage was a family tree of early insurgent leaders.

Twenty years after the revolution many of the murals could do with a fresh coat of paint. León's civic leaders are strapped for cash, but local cobbler Marvin Mendoza has started his own drive to save the historic images. "People are more close minded now," Marvin griped when I asked about his one-man crusade. "I get very little support. I have to get out there myself and repaint the murals. But I have dedicated myself to recording the past, so that young people won't forget and it won't happen again."

To that end, Marvin has also transformed his shoe-repair shop into a museum of the revolution, an oddball collection that includes military gear, yellowed old newspapers and photos of various "heroes," ranging from Ho Chi Minh to Pope John Paul II to 1970s disco diva Donna Summer. Dressed in jungle fatigues and army boots, his long black hair tied back in a ponytail, Marvin flipped through his scrapbook. "This is me," he said, pointing to a black-and-white photo of a teenager throwing stones at soldiers. "This building belonged to the military in those days. We had to burn down a big wooden door to get in and throw them out."

León's alter ego, the old colonial city of Granada, lounges along the Pan American Highway about an hour's drive south of Managua. Granada has always been conservative and quiet. During the revolution its citizens were more likely to side with right-wing dictator Anastasio Somoza than with the Sandinistas. And, while the people of León seemed to have turned their backs on the past, the good citizens of Granada have turned history into a profit-making venture.

Most of the elderly buildings around the Parque Colón have been handsomely restored, cafés offer alfresco dining beneath the stars, and horse-drawn carriages clop along the cobblestone streets that run down to the lake. Daily life also retains a certain bygone charm. Residents throw their front doors open after dark, drag their wicker rocking chairs onto the sidewalks, and chat with their neighbors. The local mortuary conducts funerals with a horse-drawn hearse, the driver decked out in a stovepipe hat, the horses clad in white mesh blankets.

Even the factories harken back to another century. On the grounds of the Reyes Cigar Company I found workers making stogies at wooden

Day's catch resting on her head, Tina Vanegas-Busillo *heads for the market stalls along Torolla Beach in eastern El Salvador. Although the government encourages tourists to visit its Pacific beaches, the local economy still relies on shrimp in winter and fish in summer.*

Following pages: *Independence Day parade thunders down the Pan American Highway in San Salvador, the heavy military presence symbolic of El Salvador's turbulent modern history. Though independent since 1821, the small country suffers unremitting poverty and political instability.*

SUNRISE HIGHLIGHTS a neighborhood in Tegucigalpa. The Honduran metropolis shares two traits with most other Central American capitals: It nestles in a valley surrounded by high mountains—and it monopolizes the nation's political and economic power.

tables set around a sunny courtyard. They would choose about six leaves, carefully prune the ends with a disk-shaped knife and roll them into a rough cigar with the palms of their hands. It took on average about three minutes per cigar. About once an hour the workers would take a short break, dancing merengue steps around the courtyard to the sound of Latin music.

"Our tobacco is grown in Estelí, up in the highlands in northern Nicaragua," said Yesenia Gonzalez, the 25-year-old factory manager. "We did an experiment last year of growing tobacco on a farm near the Pan American Highway not far from Granada. And we're also starting to buy from small farmers on the islands in Lake Nicaragua. We prefer to do a mixture of tobacco from all the different areas, and this has proved to be an excellent blend." The company is also experimenting with different flavors: vanilla, chocolate, coffee, rum, and piña colada cigars. "Chocolate is my favorite," Yesenia grinned. "Rum cigars make you a little dizzy from the alcohol."

Nearly all of Reyes cigars are bound for the U.S., where they are sold under various brand names, including the personal label of legendary football coach Mike Ditka, who led the Chicago Bears to Super Bowl victory in 1986. Yesenia produced a Ditka stogie, much longer that the others and with its own special band: a reproduction of Ditka's diamond-studded Super Bowl ring. "He has them custom made for his family and friends and players on his team," Yesenia explained. "He's never been down here, but we are hoping that he comes to Nicaragua very soon."

Another American pastime—baseball—has grown into the national sport since its introduction early in the 20th century by invading U.S. Marines. (They were safeguarding American efforts to build a canal across Nicaragua that never happened.) Every large city has a professional team, but it would be difficult to find a more dramatic setting than the home diamond in Masaya: Roberto Clemente Stadium perches on the edge of a steep cliff overlooking Lake Masaya; a volcano puffs on the opposite shore. As we took our seats, a volcanic rumble shook the grandstand.

San Fernando, the Masaya home team, took an early lead, but the real action was off the field. The Granada ball boy kept himself busy by sprinkling everything—bats, balls, gloves—with some sort of magic powder that was supposed to make his team play better. A Brazilian-style samba band pounded out a steady beat every time a San Fernando batter stepped to the plate. Vendors with metal trays and plastic buckets balanced on their heads plied the aisles, calling out the names of various snacks: fried cheese sticks, meat pastries, salted orange slices, even shots of rum. Mariano bought at least one of everything, relishing the food as much as the game.

Around the third inning, the announcer interrupted his play-by-play: "Ladies and gentlemen, we have a very special guest tonight. Please welcome Major Leaguer Dennis Martinez." That sent a buzz through the crowd. The most famous Nicaraguan athlete of all time, maybe the best

CHRISTMAS FIREWORKS LIGHT GRANADA'S *Palacio Episcopal, as revelers parade a statue of the Virgin around the main square. Nicaragua's oldest Spanish colonial city, Granada perches beside windswept Lake Nicaragua, its fine colonial architecture still an ornament to the lakeshore.*

OPPOSITE: *Up since dawn, a young lady of Granada kneels in the city's massive cathedral before her first communion. A major event in the lives of children, the communion celebration culminates with a parade and street party.*

Howler monkeys *occupy treetop habitats in the dense tropical forests along the Río Corobicí in northern Costa Rica.*

Opposite: *Solitary* sabanero *rides the range in Costa Rica's Guanacaste Province, heartland of the traditional cowboy and colonial cultures.*

baseball player ever to come out of Central America, someone who had pitched in both World Series and All-Star Games, was sitting not 50 feet away from me. "He grew up in Granada," said a fan sitting behind me. "This was his first team." Martinez was being deluged by well-wishers, including Mariano, who left with an autographed baseball cap.

The following morning I bid Mariano a reluctant farewell and watched his pickup truck pull away from Granada on the first leg of his return journey to Guatemala. Minutes later I hopped a bus to Costa Rica, a route that took me along the western shore of Lake Nicaragua to Peñas Blancas. It proved to be the most troublesome border crossing of my entire journey through Latin America. Everyone stood in line for almost 90 minutes to get stamped out of Nicaragua. Then we reboarded the bus, drove about a mile across a no-man's-land, and stood in line for another hour to get stamped into Costa Rica.

I assumed that was the end of the formalities, but our driver appeared, looking rather perturbed. "The customs guy says that unless every passenger pays him a hundred colones, he will make us take everything out and search every piece of baggage on this bus," he announced solemnly. "You must decide among yourselves." It was the equivalent of 50 cents in U.S. currency, not much to me but maybe the other passengers would feel differently. Across the parking lot, customs officials and their sniffer dogs

were rifling through the luggage from another coach. Nobody on our bus said a word, but the course of action was obvious. Everyone coughed up a hundred colones when the customs man appeared, even the nun sitting in front of me. All told, he collected about $16.

RANCHES SPRAWL ON BOTH SIDES of the Pan American Highway in northern Costa Rica's Guanacaste province. One of Central America's most distinctive and individualistic pockets, Guanacaste is home to *sabaneros*—cowboys who have always considered themselves different from their countrymen. Their ancestors were among the earliest European pioneers in Central America, settling the region in the late 16th century. When the region broke away from Spanish rule in the 1820s, Guanacaste nearly became a small independent state wedged between Nicaragua and Costa Rica. In the end, locals voted to become part of Costa Rica, but the province remains a very distinctive region culturally.

Although most of the region is flat, a chain of volcanoes slithers up its eastern flank, a primeval landscape of smoldering cinder cones and cloud forests that harbors more plant and animal species per acre than any other part of the Americas. Much of the landscape is now protected within the confines of national parks, which form the foundation of Costa Rica's ecotourism thrust, the most aggressive in Latin America. One of the most impressive parks is Rincón de la Vieja, a composite volcano with nine different eruptive spots, or craters, that last blew its top in 1998. The name means "corner of the old lady" in Spanish, but nobody I asked was quite sure how the mountain got that tag. One legend centers around a Spanish matriarch who lived by herself at the base of the volcano in the late 18th century. Another story has overtones of Romeo and Juliet: A young Spanish lady, who, spurned by her lover's family, lived out the rest of her days on the mountain, turning her back on a conservative colonial society that had destroyed her romance. Either way, Rincón de la Vieja is a haunting and highly beautiful place with bubbling mud pools, hot springs, tropical dry forests, lush rain forests, and myriad wildlife. Happily, nearby haciendas welcome overnight visitors.

I mounted a chestnut steed at Buena Vista Hacienda and followed sabanero José Morales across rolling grassland to mud baths and hot springs on the western edge of the national park. "It's very hot mud, easy to burn yourself," José told me, scooping a handful of muck from a ceramic vat. "People say it's good for your skin because of the volcanic minerals. I use it daily myself, put it all over my body. It keeps my skin soft."

Following José's instructions, I spread the thick gray sludge over nearly every inch of my body. Sprawling on the nearby grass, I let the mud dry to the consistency of chalk, then I sank into the hot springs. I can't say whether or not the treatment cured whatever might have been ailing me, but it did produce the sort of calm that normally settles over my body after

I've had a good massage. As we lounged in the balmy water, José talked about his life as a sabanero. "My job now is working with horses and cows. But when I was younger, I used to ride bulls a lot. Obviously, sometimes you fall off the bull. But it's like riding a horse—you fall off and get up and try again." His mouth widened into a broad grin. "But I would say that in my time, I have stayed on more than I have fallen off."

José told me that Guanacaste has changed immeasurably during his 42 years. "When I was a boy, I never imagined that so many people would come here to see the land, so many tourists. But I see this as a good thing: Tourism allows us to protect our environment." A troupe of howler monkeys struck up a loud chorus in the nearby forest, announcing the forthcoming sunset. The Pacific Ocean glistened like molten silver as we rode back across the range, headed for a guest hacienda. It could not have been a more enchanting evening.

I tanked up in Guanacaste's capital, the sleepy crossroads town of Liberia. Its chalky soil and whitewashed houses have earned it the name Ciudad Blanca, White City. Beyond it, the Pan American was flanked by spacious ranches, where zebu cattle grazed on rich savanna grass. The highway hurdled the fast-flowing Río Corobicí on one of the original Pan American Highway bridges, a simple steel span erected in the 1940s but still strong enough to shoulder hundreds of vehicles each day.

Just beyond the bridge was Las Pumas Wildlife Center, an animal orphanage that houses a number of rare or endangered tropical cat species, including jaguars, pumas, jaguarundis, and ocelots. Lilly Bodmer de Hagnauer, a transplanted Swiss, started the center in 1967 with a single margay, a small spotted wild cat indigenous to Costa Rica. "There is still a lot of hunting and poaching in Costa Rica," Lilly explained as we peered through chicken wire at one of her resident jaguars. "That won't change for three or four generations, until people are educated about the reasons why they shouldn't kill these animals." Startled by our voices, the big cat slowly opened its golden eyes. Then, seeing that it was only Lilly, it went back to sleep.

The cats at Las Pumas are either orphaned babies whose parents were killed by poachers or else exotic pets that became too big and dangerous to live in ordinary homes. Lilly's original goal was to release them back into the wild and then track them by radio to record their range and behavior. However, she is now hesitant about liberating cats, because they are usually shot nearly as fast as she releases them. The disappearance of the cats' natural habitat has created the violent interface that now exists between these animals and the human environment. "A jaguar recently attacked and killed 14 calves at a dairy farm near here," Lilly told me. "We built a trap and tried to catch it, but the cat was too smart for that. We tried tranquilizers next but we couldn't get close enough to it."

With problems like these between wild cats and humans, the center's captive-breeding program has been put on hold. "What will I do with the babies?" Lilly lamented.

IN DARIÉN PROVINCE, the far eastern part of Panama, the Pan American Highway degenerates from smooth pavement into muddy track, culminating in jungle that can only be negotiated by foot or canoe. Renting a four-wheel-drive vehicle in Panama City, I drove down to Darién with photographer Susie Post and Abigail Grajales. An Emberá Indian guide, he is also a member of a national organization that strives to protect indigenous rights. "My people are very worried about what will happen to our land if the Pan American Highway is paved beyond the Río Bayano," Abigail told me as we drove south from the capital. "We are also worried that new roads will be built from the Pan American down to the rivers, something that could further endanger our resources and way of life." His greatest concerns were illegal logging and property speculation—people from the city buying up huge blocks of land for ranches and farms. That anxiety seemed well founded as we rolled down the highway. Much of the once pristine region was already deforested, the trees replaced by rice farms and rangeland for cattle.

The Pan American leaps the Río Bayano on a sturdy steel bridge erected in 1974. At the eastern end of the span I found a bronze plaque with a moving inscription: "The government of Panama honors the memory of those who gave their lives to connect North and South America." But truth be told, the connection was never made. While strategic considerations—like the possibility of an enemy attack on the Panama Canal—spurred the U.S. government to fund the completion of various breaches in the Pan American Highway, the Darién Gap was never filled. Today it remains the only stretch between northern Mexico and southern Argentina that cannot be negotiated by motor vehicles.

Beyond the bridge, the tarmac ends abruptly. Outside a sleepy little jungle town called Meteti, the road is impassable during the rainy season and virtually impossible without four-wheel drive during the rest of the year. Beyond the village of Yaviza there is nothing but water and trees, the 65-mile knot of jungle called the Darién Gap that thwarted engineers for more than half a century. Today's modern construction techniques could easily cleave the jungle and force the Pan American Highway through to Colombia. Now, though, the primary barriers to completing the route are political and environmental concerns.

Alfonso Moreno, local director of ProDarién, a government agency charged with developing economic sustainability in the remote region, faces this dilemma on a daily basis. He admits that paving the existing highway would provide several benefits. "Yes, there would be progress," he told me. "Progress in communications, health care, and education. It would open doors and channels to improve (Continued on page 84)

(Continued on page 84)

On the Panama Canal, *two cargo ships enter the Miraflores Locks, last leg of their canal voyage from the Atlantic to the Pacific. Still one of the world's great engineering wonders, the 51-mile-long waterway through the Isthmus of Panama was completed in 1914. In 1999 the canal passed from American to Panamanian control.*

Following pages: *Heading for the bush, a zebu steer tries to elude its cowboy pursuer along an unpaved stretch of the Pan American in eastern Panama.*

INDIAN MOTHER *prepares her daughter for a tribal dance ceremony at Peña Bijagual, a Chocó village on the banks of the Río Tiura in the Darién Gap. The Chocó remain largely untouched by the 20th century, living in thatched huts and surviving on the bounty of the surrounding jungle.*

our lives. But regulations should be in place before they start paving to guarantee the lifestyles, culture, and environment of Darién."

As we stood at the very end of the road, a muddy bank above the Río Tuira, Alfonso described the negative backlash that came after the unpaved highway was pushed through to Yaviza in the 1980s. "Many people came from other areas of Panama. They cut down the virgin forests and started farming, but the land was only fertile for a few years, so they cut down more forest. Also, Colombians are already coming across our border, cutting down trees and illegally mining," Alfonso lamented. "I can't imagine how much more they would harm our environment if there was a highway for them to use. What would become of our forest and fauna? For now, I think the Pan American Highway should end here. If not, our problems will just be aggravated."

The following morning we boarded a motorized dugout canoe and headed up the river into territory that would be deeply impacted if the highway were ever completed. Our destination was Peña Bijagual, a Chocó Indian village largely untouched by 20th-century civilization, several dozen thatch-roofed huts perched on stilts along the river. No electricity or running water, no televisions or cell phones. Standard dress is basically nothing (although missionaries taught the Chocó women to cover their naked bodies in the presence of visitors).

The villagers told me that the Pan American Highway had so far had very little effect on their lives. "We are creating our own progress," said Viviana Guaemora, head of a women's handicraft cooperative called the Kiosco So Bia (Kiosk of Good Faith). The co-op members make intricately woven baskets and wooden carvings to raise money for the local school, three rooms beneath a thatched roof where students are taught in a combination of Chocó and Spanish.

Two of the basket weavers, Filadelphia Rosales and her daughter Nimia Teocama, invited me into their hut. Their baskets were lovely, made from palm leaves tinted with jungle vegetable dyes. I was especially intrigued by the insect design on Nimia's basket. "It's lice," she explained with a straight face. "You know, the bugs that get into your hair." She waited for the shock to register on my face and then let out a deep belly laugh, pleased with her joke. It was really a water bug design.

Nimia begged me to purchase her handiwork. "If you don't buy my basket, I won't have money to buy clothes at the shops in town. I'll have to walk around naked!" she asserted. Another Indian joke, because as soon as we were gone from the village, their T-shirts and shorts would be quickly cast aside. Au naturel was the fashion of choice.

It was refreshing to have met such guileless people in such a splendid natural setting. As we headed back to Yaviza, I found myself agreeing with those who think the Darién Gap should remain untouched, the only broken thread in the long path of the Pan American.

END OF THE LINE, *the village of Yaviza sits at the southern terminus of the Pan American Highway through Central America. Here in eastern Panama, the highway's long path south is interrupted by the Darién Gap, a jungle wilderness accessible only by boat. On the far side of the gap, the highway picks up again in South America.*

COLOMBIA AND ECUADOR

PHOTOGRAPHS BY SUSIE POST

After the Darién Gap interlude, the Pan American Highway picks up steam again in the remote northwest corner of Colombia. Beyond the eastern banks of the Río Atrato, it climbs into the deeply wooded hills at the northern extreme of the Andes. This rather humble terrain heralds the beginning of the world's longest mountain system, a land filled with sky-searing volcanoes and enigmatic valleys.

For most of its long and winding route through Colombia, the highway clings to the highlands, literally marking a path into the clouds. At first glance this seems like a rather foolish course. Wouldn't it have been easier to forge a path along the Pacific coast? Back in the 1930s, engineers considered the same question and quickly discerned that the jungle along Colombia's western shore was nearly as impenetrable as the Darién Gap. History was also on their side. The area's most advanced pre-Colombian civilizations took root in the highlands and the Spanish conquistadors followed their lead, virtually ignoring the Pacific littoral in favor of the Andes.

Flying into Medellín, the largest city in northwest Colombia, I made inquiries about traveling to the exact spot where the Pan American Highway starts anew. The looks I got were warning enough. Locals obviously thought I was crazy even to consider the trip. It wasn't the jungle they feared but rather the human denizens that now inhabit the border region, an often deadly combination of left-wing guerrillas, right-wing paramilitary groups, and good old-fashioned bandits.

The frontier region remains a remote and forbidding place. For all intents and purposes, the central government has no control. "That end of the Pan American Highway is oil and banana country—that's what the guerrillas and paramilitary are fighting over," explained a Medellín-based doctor whose work has taken her to many dubious parts of Colombia.

Nearly everyone I quizzed said it would be a foolhardy trip. With blond hair and fair skin, I was a prime candidate for abduction (several people suggested, quite seriously, that I dye my hair black). The guerrillas would kidnap me to stimulate publicity for their cause; the bandits would hold me for a huge ransom; the paramilitary (Continued on page 95)

D*URING A FESTIVAL CELEBRATING* F*REDONIA'S FOUNDING,* *the town's normally placid streets throb with music and dance. Founded in 1830, the city is one of Colombia's oldest coffee towns and still a major supplier of top-quality beans.*

P*RECEDING PAGES:* *Permanently capped in snow and ice, 19,347-foot Cotopaxi, one of the world's highest active volcanoes, hovers in the clouds above central Ecuador. Not far from the Pan American Highway, this crown jewel of the tumultuous highland region known as the Avenue of the Volcanoes roared to life with its last major eruption in 1975.*

TRAFFIC SNARLED AND HIGH-RISE FLANKED, *Plazuela Nutibara epitomizes the renaissance of Medellín. Since the demise of the big drug cartels in the early 1990s, Colombia's second largest city has rebuilt its economy around legitimate manufacturing and trade.*

IN MEDELLÍN'S BARRIO TRISTE, *homeless addicts inhabit an abandoned apartment building called the "cave." Although the city's reputation as a narco-traffic center has subsided in recent years, lingering spin-offs from the drug trade remain a pressing social problem.*

OPPOSITE: *Genifer Arteago Gil celebrates her 15th birthday with a street party in Barrio Triste. Addicted to shoe glue at birth, Genifer is one of numerous orphans and abandoned children who live on Medellín's inner-city streets.*

FROM A MIST-SHROUDED RIDGE above the city two Medellín architects—and their canine companions—contemplate the modern metropolis.

OPPOSITE: Founded by European immigrants in the 18th century, Medellín sprawls across the fertile Aburrá Valley, the urban centerpiece of the country's coffee-growing region.

would probably just shoot me. So I hunkered down in Medellín, a city once synonymous with serious trouble but now a bastion of tranquility amid the chaos that dominates modern Colombia. In the 1980s, Medellín was the most notorious metropolis in the Western Hemisphere, home of the drug lord Pablo Escobar Gaviria and his cartel. Using murder and mayhem as business tools, they fashioned the city into a thriving narcotics marketplace. But Escobar's empire came crashing down in 1993, when he was killed in an army ambush. Since then, Medellín has slowly returned to peace and prosperity, a resurrection that manifests itself in construction projects, a flourishing arts scene, and local pride.

"People here are very proud of being from Medellín," said Juan Sabaneta, a fashion photographer I met in the Parque de los Periodistas, a nightly gathering place for young people. "They really have a drive to succeed, to make money, to make business, even if they are poor. That's one reason why the Medellín cartel was so successful." I got a similar line from Jorge Salazar, one of Juan's companions and a professor of architecture at the Universidad Nacional: "We are always making plans for the future, and we are brilliant at making business. That is the basic factor that makes this city different."

Medellín sits at the bottom of the deep *(Continued on page 100)*

BREAKFAST OF RICE, TORTILLAS, AND HOT CHOCOLATE *fuels workers at a coffee plantation astride the Pan American between Neira and Chinchiná. World's second largest coffee grower after Brazil, Colombia produces more than ten million bags of beans each year, most slated for export. Pickers can be as young as ten-year-old Carlos Rios (opposite), who spends long days harvesting the ripe beans.*

FOLLOWING PAGES: *Amid the sometimes violent volcanic landscape of northern Ecuador, Lago de San Pablo serenely captures cloud reflections. Through these Ecuadoran highlands, the Pan American follows a former royal road of the Inca.*

Aburrá Valley. The Andes rise more than 3,000 feet on either side, their peaks often shrouded in billowy clouds that create an almost alpine climate. But the weather on the valley floor is subtropical. Humid days fade into warm evenings that bring most of the city's two million inhabitants onto the streets. But the city cannot quite escape its nefarious past, as I discovered in Barrio Triste. A tough neighborhood on the edge of downtown Medellín, it lies just a stone's throw away from the Pan American Highway. The area's daylight activity centers around auto and truck repair, carried out in scores of shops. But after dark, Barrio Triste becomes the haunt of the homeless, prostitutes, and junkies, many of them children. One of the few people who dwells in both worlds is Giovanny Patiño, a 30-year-old brake mechanic and self-styled godfather of local street kids.

Giovanny invited me into his home, a windowless, one-room apartment adjacent to his father's brake shop. The decor was truly bizarre: A cow's head crowned with a blond wig, mismatched car lights arranged in geometric patterns, and a chrome guitar made from old bumpers—a reflection of Giovanny's own peculiar life. "I grew up among bandits, beggars, and prostitutes," he told me with no hint of shame. "I became a delinquent, and I went to jail. When I was in jail, I started to think about my situation. I was very humiliated, and I decided that when I got out, I would help people in the street." He kept his pledge, collecting free medicine for the homeless, organizing soccer games between the addicts and mechanics, trying to protect the street kids from prostitution and other vices.

Giovanny took me to a two-story apartment building long ago abandoned by its owners and seized by street people. Like a vision from Dante's Inferno, the "Cave," as it's called, exposed a mosaic of human suffering. Scores of people lived in dank rooms that stank of garbage and feces, their bodies racked by AIDS and other maladies, many of them smoking marijuana or *bazuco,* a local form of crack cocaine. Near the entrance, a woman sold cigarettes from a wooden tray, needle marks running up her arms, her faced covered in cold sores. Teenagers shared hits from plastic bottles filled with shoe glue—the only drug they could afford. At the end of a corridor, beneath a statue of the Virgin Mary, two young boys sprawled in hammocks, their eyes glazed from drugs.

Yet amid this despair, I found kindness and hope. An old man with a gray beard appeared through a broken window. When he lunged at me, I recoiled. But he just wanted to shake my hand, welcome a rare visitor to his alien world. Another man, both arms severed at the elbows in a train accident, insisted that I visit his room. Tiny and dark, it was furnished with items salvaged from trash dumps: an aged stove, a battered television, a rickety wooden bed, and plastic lighters arranged in a rainbow across the wall. Smiling from ear to ear, the armless man was about as house proud as anyone could be. That's when I realized why they call this Barrio Triste— Sad Neighborhood. It's the kind of place that makes you want to cry.

UNABLE TO TRAVEL TO THE NORTHWEST, I appeased my wanderlust by exploring other parts of the Pan American network, tentacles that have been added since the original roadway was built in the 1930s. One of these spurs runs southeast of Medellín, through the Cordillera Central down to the Río Magdalena, then up into the mountains again. It terminates finally at Bogotá. Much of Colombia's flower industry has taken root along this stretch, a budding export business that sends millions of bouquets each year to U.S. florists.

Cultivos Miramonte is one of the largest growers, 111 acres of chrysanthemums, sunflowers, asters, and other flowers quilting a valley near Río Negro. "Flower farming started about 25 years ago in this area," said Victoria Cortes, an agronomist at Miramonte, "when somebody noticed that chrysanthemums grow faster here than on the Pampas around Bogotá." Victoria's tour of the Miramonte estate revealed an amazingly sophisticated operation, with drip irrigation, cableways with plastic buckets to transport cut flowers from the fields, and fertilizer that was a blend of chicken manure and compost rather than chemicals.

"We try to be as organic as possible," Victoria explained. "Otherwise in ten years, the soil will be dead." Flowers are cut and delivered to various wholesalers in the Miami area the same day, first trucked along the Pan American then flown out of Medellín in refrigerated containers. The normal load is 24,000 bunches a day, but Miramonte's exports peak at 40,000 bunches a day during such American holidays as Valentine's Day and Easter.

South of Medellín along the Pan American, the Zona Cafetera is the soul of Colombia's coffee country. Conditions are nearly perfect for coffee cultivation—rich volcanic soil, abundant sunshine, plentiful rain, and elevations between 2,000 and 5,000 feet. Since the late 19th century, coffee has been the country's leading export. Today, Fredonia is typical of the coffee towns that dot the region. The little brown beans are an abiding local obsession, and the favorite pastime of many Fredonians is sipping freshly brewed Colombian in one of the outdoor cafés that ring the town square. A cup of coffee costs the equivalent of a mere 15 cents—the best java I tasted along the entire length of the Pan American.

Exploring the narrow back streets of Fredonia, I came upon a flurry of activity at a coffee warehouse, as workmen loaded burlap bags full of beans onto the back of a truck. "There are four arrobas in each bag," said warehouse owner Carlos Velez. "Each arroba is 25 U.S. pounds. This is not the metric system but an old tradition we've been using forever, the old Spanish style of measuring." This shipment was bound for export, probably to the U.S. via a middleman in Medellín. Carlos jabbed a long tube-like instrument into each coffee bag and examined the beans for quality. "Coffee is better if it's lighter," he continued. "Darker beans are no good, what we call *pasilla,* low-quality coffee." *(Continued on page 106)*

R<small>ECALCITRANT</small> <small>PIG TAKES ON</small> <small>THREE MEN</small> trying to coax it across the Pan American Highway at Otavalo, in northern Ecuador. Each Saturday as dawn breaks, a lively animal market fills this traditional Indian town with barnyard bleats and grunts and the sound of human bargaining.

Following pages: Mountain stream on the outskirts of Otavalo makes a convenient laundry spot for a local Indian family. The flowing skeins of wool will be woven into ponchos, blankets, and clothing on back-strap looms, a weaving process almost unchanged for 400 years.

Coffee isn't the only thing for which the central Colombia highlands are famous. The stretch of the Pan American Highway between Medellín and Santa Bárbara is often part of the annual Tour de Colombia, arguably the most important bicycle race in South America. But on any given Sunday hundreds of brightly clad cyclists toil up the inclines and whiz down into the valleys, some rehearsing for the big event, others simply getting some exercise. Bikers who get a flat don't have to worry, because every little hamlet seems to boast a rubber vendor. In a tiny place called Gauyabo, Nelson Rodriguez cuts up old tires with a kitchen carving knife then fuses the strips together with an old-fashioned flatiron. On the day I stopped at his shop, he was making rubber linings for truck tires, but his repertoire also included playground swings, plant pots, and furniture stuffing—all made from recycled tires. "On many roads around the country, people are now surviving this way," Nelson told me. "In this town there are four other people doing the same thing."

Along much of this route, the Pan American clings like a vine to the mountainsides, and at several points it threads a razor's edge along the lofty ridges that divide the Magdalena and Cauca valleys. The vistas (and vertigo) are truly amazing, a panorama of deep ravines and mist-shrouded mountains, nearly every slope smothered in dark green coffee bushes. For the most part, the highlands highway follows the same route that European settlers blazed in the mid-1800s, when the Zona Cafetera was first settled. It was tough going, hacking through the thick forests that covered central Colombia in those days. Some pioneer communities were cut off from civilization for years because of the rugged terrain, pockets of fair-skinned people in the middle of the South American wilderness. The second generation of pioneers was the first to cultivate coffee, forging the central highlands into one of Latin America's most prosperous regions.

That prosperity is most evident in places like Manizales, a former coffee town that has burgeoned into a city of some 350,000. With tightly packed houses and office buildings perched on hillsides—plus a cool damp climate—Manizales bears more than a passing resemblance to San Francisco. There isn't much left from colonial times. Income from coffee production has been plowed back into modern buildings and civic improvements. The city has a flashy restaurant row and some of Colombia's best-dressed citizens. Imported sports utility vehicles and pickup trucks cruise the streets. The thriving local economy has also allowed Manizales to avoid much of the drug and political violence that has plagued Colombia over the past 30 years.

Yet the city is not without its demons. Towering above the skyline is snow-mantled Nevado del Ruiz, the country's most notorious volcano. It looks tranquil enough during idle periods, when it forms the centerpiece of a national park popular with climbers and trekkers. But the mountain can explode with stupendous fury.

It last erupted, tragically, in 1985, during the night when people were sleeping. Pyroclastic flows and mud slides sweeping down the mountain's eastern slopes killed more than 23,000 souls. Fifteen years later, few signs of the disaster remain. The fields around Chinchiná are abundant again with bright yellow beans waiting to be harvested.

The *chapoleros,* or coffee pickers, work a ten-hour day, with short breaks for breakfast and lunch. They get paid 120 pesos (12 cents) a kilo. One of them told me he figures the average worker picks about a hundred kilos a day. "You know the coffee is ripe," he said, "if you squeeze the husk and the bean jumps out. That means a machine can peel off the pulp with no problem. If I pick green beans, I might get fired."

Another city that owes its success to the tasty little bean is Pereira, at the southern edge of the Zona Cafetera. The highway flows into town on a brand-new, steel-cable bridge across the Río Otún, at just over a mile one of the longest spans along the entire length of the Pan American. Beyond Pereira, the highway lunges out of the highlands and down into the steamy valley of the Río Cauca. Almost at once the climate turns tropical, and coffee gives way to vast sweeps of sugarcane and citrus. Even the language is different. No longer the fast-paced *paisa* accent of Medellín and the coffee country, it slows into a sultry Spanish that matches the flatland heat and humidity. The highway also changes, evolving from a sinuous two-lane road into an arrow-straight, four-lane expressway flanked by huge agribusiness concerns.

The towns of the Cauca Valley are much older than any in the adjacent highlands: Cali was founded in 1536, Cartago in 1540, Buga in 1650. Yet they are not without their relics. In Cartago I came across the remnants of a narrow-gauge railroad, the chief link between Medellín and Cali before the 1940s. Overgrown with weeds, the line is no longer in use, a reflection of the sorry state of the railroad industry throughout much of Latin America. The Pan American Highway, in league with modern air transport, has made the Iron Horse obsolete.

I rolled into Buga at the height of the pilgrimage season, when thousands of people flock to the Basílica del Señor de los Milagros, where Jesus is believed to have appeared to a local woman 400 years ago. With pastel buildings and stone churches set around leafy squares, Buga had much more of an antique feel than most Colombian towns I'd come across. It also yielded the only smuggler I would meet during two weeks in Colombia, a taxi driver who trafficked in black market auto parts and tires from Ecuador, hidden beneath potato sacks in the flatbed of his truck. "The potatoes pay for the gas and road tolls," he declared, proud of his own cleverness. "Everything on top is pure profit."

At the southern end of the Cauca Valley, Cali basks in tropical heat, its nearly two million people making it the country's second largest metropolis. It was little more than a sleepy *(Continued on page 114)*

TEENAGE NEWLYWEDS *Veronica Cando and Jesus Lema celebrate their marriage in Otavalo, where couples typically wed early in life. Indigenous peoples, like the Otavalenos, still account for the vast majority of Andes inhabitants.*

OLDER WEDDING GUEST *proudly wears a trademark necklace. Otavaleno women spend a lifetime amassing glass beads, even purchasing coveted imported strands from central Europe.*

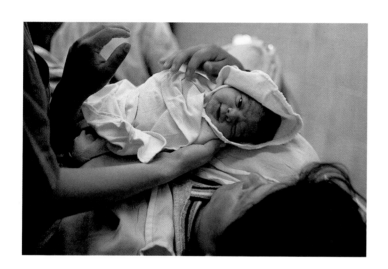

SHOESHINE BOYS OF QUITO *gather in the plaza fronting the Monastery of San Francisco. Construction of the imposing baroque landmark, Ecuador's oldest church, began just weeks after the Spanish founded the city in 1534. Lying almost at the zero parallel, Quito derives its name from the Spanish word for Equator. Opposite: Melania Mallama reaches out for her newborn daughter at Quito's Gineco-Obstétrico Isidro Ayora Hospital, which delivers more babies than any other hospital in the city—a total of 11,540 in 1998.*

FOLLOWING PAGES: *Spotlight beams across an audience of thousands packed into Quito's Teatro Agora for a concert featuring a Spanish crooner and a local Ecuadoran group—a combination that reflects the city's heritage.*

provincial town until a railroad linked it in the early 20th century to the port of Buenaventura on the Pacific coast and to Medellín in the north. Cali's heyday soon followed, as the city reaped the benefits of both a rich agricultural hinterland and a rapidly growing industrial base. Nowadays, Cali revolves around factories and feet—spirited salsa clubs called *grills*, where residents dance the night away. Despite its high spirits, the city is still plagued by drug cartels, including the infamous Cali cartel.

South of Cali, as the Pan American begins its slow ascent into the Andes again, the European-based society that dominates central Colombia gradually gives way to traditional Indian ways. The trend continues across the border in Ecuador, which harbors one of the largest Indian populations in South America. Not far into Ecuador sits the famous market town of Otavalo, where I lingered for a day—shopping, eating, and watching the ruddy-faced Indians in their bowler hats. The Otavalenos have been famous for their weaving since pre-Columbian days, spinning llama, alpaca, and sheep wools into an amazing array of shawls, blankets, ponchos, sweaters, and wall hangings. After browsing the stalls, I ducked into one of the town's trendy cafés, a scrumptious spin-off of the tourist boom. My waitress, a young blond from Arizona, reeled off a menu straight out of Berkeley or Seattle. I settled for a slice of Black Forest cake and a cappuccino.

The countryside around Otavalo was equally appetizing—rolling, green hills framed in snowy peaks and navy blue lakes. The Otavalenos believe they are descended from the union of two of these peaks and that the lakes are tears shed by their volcano mother because her offspring could never get along—a legend that explains both creation and the intertribal warfare that once plagued this region.

In the shadow of these mountains and along the shores of these lakes are modest mud-brick villages with cobblestone streets that produce the treasures for Otavalo's market. Beneath the thatched roof of a workshop in Peguche, I watched in wonder as a young weaver created an alpaca masterpiece, a sweater in deep earth tones. I couldn't leave without making a small purchase—a cardigan for my wife. Up the road, in the leather town of Cotacachi, I was faced with a similar scene. The wallet came out again.

I pulled into San Rafaél just as the annual village fiesta was about to kick off, a bizarre and wondrous spectacle that blended Christian ritual and lingering respect for Inti, the ancient Inca sun god. The entire population of San Rafaél, several hundred people, had gathered in a muddy field on the edge of the Pan American. Everyone was dressed to the nines, the women in fluffy blouses and hand-embroidered shawls, the men in threadbare suits, the kids in clown costumes and mock military uniforms. The mayor was there too, his face perched beneath a funny little hat, arm-in-arm with the town beauty queen. Leading the festivities were two costumed men: a white-faced clown called Coraza and a black-faced demon called Diablo Huma, regional embodiments of good and evil. Both dispensed moonshine to the crowd. The hooch came in two varieties: *chica,* fermented corn liquor served in gourds; and *chauarmishqui,* a clear, agave-based drink guzzled from recycled whiskey bottles. Both went down like battery acid.

Music poured from two bands, a police ensemble with brass instruments and a traditional Andean quintet. They struck up a joint tune, and many villagers joined a slow and sinuous conga line that snaked its way through the crowd. Teenagers ignited fireworks perched atop long bamboo poles, and the villagers started to shout: "Viva Otavalo! Viva Pueblo! Viva San Rafaél!" Everyone fell in behind the bands, dancing and shouting all the way up a cobblestone street to the mud-brick village church, where they placed offerings before a statue of their patron saint.

Leaving the Indians to their revelry, I continued south along one of the more breathtaking portions of the Pan American. The scenery was wonderful, sweeping panoramas of snow-capped volcanoes, deep chasms, and distant rivers that sparkled in the Andes sun. Just before Quito, I crossed the point where the highway intersects the Equator, marked by a small stone monument. A couple of miles farther west, I found a much more grandiose geographic shrine, a stout brick tower called Mitad del Mundo, Middle of the World. From its observation deck you can look down at the invisible divide and out across the sweep of the Andes. Or you can do what all good tourists do at this spot: Pose for a snapshot with a foot in both the Northern and Southern hemispheres.

Just south of the Equator, Quito is one of the world's highest cities, sitting at 9,350 feet. Locals say they can experience four seasons in one day here, and that's not far from the truth. Nights are chilly, but the sun beats down with reckless abandon during the middle of the day. The long, narrow valleys that harbor the city are often shrouded in clouds and fog, but it rarely snows in Quito. In fact, orchids grow wild here.

Quito also happens to be the only major Andean city never destroyed by an earthquake, and much of the city's colonial heritage has survived into the 20th century. The Old Town is a treasure trove of historic churches and palaces set around cobblestone plazas where life seems to have changed little in a hundred years. San Francisco Church, the city's oldest Spanish structure, is especially evocative of the past, with its aroma of votive candles, creak of wood floors, and murmur of prayer.

Yet there is a whole different Quito in the central business district and in modern suburbs like El Valle, where flashy cars and haute couture are more the norm. One of the most striking symbols of modern Quito is the dazzling campus of San Francisco University in Cumbaya, founded in 1988 by a couple of Ecuadorian scientists who wanted to give something back to their homeland. Raising funds from corporate sources and wealthy patrons, they created a high-tech college based on the building blocks of the 21st century—medicine, engineering, business, communications, and environmental science.

Teachers are drawn from all over the world, including American ecologist Dr. Kelly Swing, who's trying to save the Amazon from his high-tech perch in the Andes. Kelly runs the university's rain forest research station at Tiputini in the Ecuadorian Amazon, but much of his work unfolds in Quito, where he lobbies government agencies and oil companies to introduce nature-friendly extraction methods.

"There is a tremendous struggle between environmental and economic interests in the Amazon," Kelly told me during a walk around the campus. "The bottom line is that gas and oil will be taken out of national parks and nature reserves. Our goal is to limit impact to one percent of the surface area." Kelly also explained that young people from indigenous tribes are being educated so that they themselves can help mediate the unavoidable tensions that arise among indigenous peoples, developers, and the government. After the tour, Kelly treated me to a slide show of the amazing flora and fauna at Tiputini. "Animals are not just present but abundant," he enthused. "You can find 200 species of trees on a one-acre plot. There is something very unique and pristine about this area."

The enduring threat to the Amazon became manifest several days later at the open-air market in Machachi, a half-day's drive south of Quito on the Pan American. A traveling *curandero,* or medicine man, had set up shop in one corner of the market, his clandestine wares spread across a dusty blanket—jaguar pelts, bear claws, toucan beaks, tapir hooves, colorful bird feathers—everything poached from the rain forest.

Speaking through a microphone attached to a small portable speaker, he extolled the virtues of various jungle remedies: "This is good for your brain, it'll make you smarter. This will cure cancer and AIDS." A large group of people had gathered around, listening intently. But when it came time to buy, they started to drift away. The curandero tried to lure them back with free samples, but the Indians wouldn't touch those either. Perhaps Kelly's message is filtering through to ordinary people.

Machachi sits in a deep furrow called the Avenue of the Volcanoes. German naturalist Alexander von Humboldt gave it that name in the early 1800s, during his marathon journey through South America. The waters of this region drain eastward, part of the Amazon watershed. As the Pan American makes its way between Quito and Cuenca, it crosses many of these streams, the only places where the highway interfaces with the Amazon Basin. I paused at one bridge, gazing down at a tiny stream. Its waters would eventually empty into the Atlantic, several thousand miles away.

Plenty of water, sunshine, and volcanic soil make the Avenue of the Volcanoes incredibly fertile. Dairy farms, cornfields, rose plantations, and wildflowers spread out on either side of the highway as I moved south. At one point I saw a herd of six llamas munching their way across a nearby hillside. They were the first of their breed that I'd seen in South America, a sign that I was moving into the Inca realm. *(Continued on page 122)*

VENEER OF SNOW MOTTLES *lava fields on the slopes of Cotopaxi. The conical volcanic peak is protected by a sprawling national park that harbors abundant Andean flora and fauna. Hikers can easily manage the volcano's lower elevations, but only experienced climbers tackle the forbidding summit.*

PLEADING FOR HANDOUTS, *a young boy hopes passengers on a cross-country bus detouring off the Pan American will take pity on his poverty. Frequent landslides in the Andes, triggered by heavy rains, often sever routes between major cities, forcing such detours.*

FOLLOWING PAGES: *On the terrace of their thatched-roof house near Cuenca, women of the Cabrera family weave Panama hats. Although the well-known headgear originated here in Ecuador, the name stems from their popularity with workers digging the Panama Canal.*

Prior to the 15th century, the Ecuadorian highlands were dominated by the Cañari people, who practiced bloody sacrificial rites. After a 17-year military campaign that kicked off in 1463, the Inca took control of the region. Their rule lasted less 50 years, but during that time they left an indelible mark on the landscape. Tomebamba (modern-day Cuenca) became the Incas' northern capital. Quito was founded as a military bastion to quell uprisings of local tribes. The two cities were connected by a royal stone road more than 20 feet wide. For a brief moment just before the Spanish conquest, the entire Inca realm—an empire that stretched from southern Colombia into northern Chile—was ruled from Ecuador.

Unlike neighboring Peru, Ecuador is rather sparse when it comes to ancient architecture. Most of the pre-Columbian temples and citadels were pulled down by the Spanish during the colonial period, to provide building materials for their cathedrals and palaces in Quito and Cuenca. But here and there, sometimes in the most unlikely places, the Inca heritage has survived. On my way to Cotopaxi National Park, I stopped off at one of those places—the Hacienda San Agustín de Callo near Latacunga. It was a rainy day and the park's famous namesake volcano was shrouded in clouds, so there was no rush. The hacienda's current owner, Mignon Plaza, ushered me into the main house. Llamas were gorging themselves on nasturtiums in the cobblestone courtyard, but not for long. Mignon whistled, and a black-and-white herd dog named Dobby appeared on the scene. He barked and nipped at the llamas' heels, and the furry creatures began to trot away—right through the middle of the house.

As we walked around the property, Mignon talked about San Agustín's long and colorful history. "Five hundred years ago there was an Inca temple on this site," she explained in English. "This house was built by the Spanish on the foundations of the temple, and some of the old Inca stonework was combined into the colonial structure." To illustrate the point, she escorted me into a large rectangular room with trapezoid stonework typical of the Inca era. "This was used as a chapel by the Spanish friars," Mignon said. "But it was once the residence of Inca chiefs."

Another Inca ruin had been converted into the hacienda dining room, where I joined Mignon for lunch. As she related more about the property's history—its days as an Augustinian convent and base camp for the 18th-century French expedition that first plotted the Equator—a flawless Andes scene was taking shape through the nearby window. The clouds had cleared, and for the first time I could see 19,347-foot Cotopaxi, one of the world's highest active volcanoes, its frosty summit glistening in the sun. Alexander von Humboldt called it "the most beautiful and regular of all the colossal peaks in the high Andes." I did not disagree. Yet within days the volcano and its lush environs would seem a distant dream, an apparition conjured by the altitude. For the Pan American Highway takes on a very different demeanor when its crosses the border into northern Peru.

WITH A THUNDERSTORM THREATENING, *donkey-borne children head for home in Vilcabamba. This area in Ecuador's deep south has gained fame as the "valley of longevity." Reputed for their long lives, the valley's inhabitants may benefit from a healthy diet, hard work, and high altitude.*

PERU AND CHILE

PHOTOGRAPHS BY MELISSA FARLOW

They lie only a few miles apart on opposite sides of the Pan American Highway, one of Peru's oldest communities and one of its newest: the mighty Chanquillo Fortress and an aspiring shantytown called Miño d'Oro. At first glance they could not be more different. Yet they are offspring of the same parents: a cultural heritage that stretches back more than 3,000 years and a harsh desert climate that dictates nearly every aspect of life along this coast.

I had been traveling in Peru for more than a week when I stumbled onto these oddball "twins" about 230 miles north of Lima. Their juxtaposition struck me as something special. Chanquillo was built about 350 B.C., although little is known about its original inhabitants. It has never been clear if the bastion was subject to real warfare or just ritual battles. Either way Chanquillo is an impressive construction, with its three concentric granite walls surrounding stocky granite towers. Whoever developed these sites, they were highly sophisticated in both architecture and worship. But an abiding mystery remains: How could they have disappeared without a trace? Were they victims of a drought caused by El Niño?

No such mystery surrounds Miño d'Oro. The inhabitants are poverty-stricken farmers who saw their homes and lands washed away during the El Niño floods of 1998. As compensation, the government granted them tracts of desert land astride the Pan American Highway, a place to rebuild their shattered lives. There wasn't much to see when I passed through on my way to Lima—20 or 30 flimsy shacks, most of them without floors or walls. But there was a lot of hope.

"We decided to call this place Miño d'Oro (Gold Mine) because of its possibilities," said Elsa Polo, a woman with big rosy cheeks who was weaving *caña brava* (wild cane) into a cover for her home. Around her swirled a flurry of activity, people digging holes, securing beams, raising roofs. "Two thousand lots have been marked off," Elsa told me. "Two thousand families will eventually live here." To fund construction, Elsa and other residents organize a roadside market every weekend, flagging down motorists with offers of hot lunches and cold drinks.

SKELETONS BLEACH *in the desert sun at Chauchilla Cemetery, a burial ground dating from the late Nazca Period (*A.D. *500-700). Grave robbers have looted most of the tombs in this remote spot in southern Peru, scattering bones, garments, and pottery shards across the blistering sands.*

PRECEDING PAGES: *Parched and windswept, Cerro la Raya overlooks the ancient city of Túcume in northern Peru. A significant Inca shrine, Túcume actually predates the Inca, its mud-brick pyramids constructed some 900 years ago.*

Huts of hope rise beside the Pan American, where farmers displaced by El Niño floods have resettled and rebuilt. The makeshift village of cane-mat shanties, christened Miño d'Oro (Gold Mine) by its optimistic founders, will eventually house some 2,000 families.

Looking around at the desert, I found it hard to believe that people could prevail against this place. The coastline here is one of the world's most desolate places, a starkly beautiful region that stretches all the way from Ecuador into northern Chile, where it merges with the even harsher Atacama. This is desert in the most extreme sense—shifting sand dunes, dry riverbeds, rocky plains, and treeless mountains. Sandstorms and dust devils are far more common than rain showers. In fact, years may pass between downpours, rendering this one of the Earth's driest stretches. Temperatures can drop to near freezing at night and easily soar above 100°F by day. Vast empty tracks support nothing, not even cactus or scrub.

Despite these ruthless conditions, the desert coast gave birth to a succession of incredible cultures—Sechín, Nazca, Mochica, Paracas, and Chimu—that predated and in many ways exceeded the mountain-dwelling Inca. Oasis valleys fed by snowmelt from the Andes provided the sustenance of life, each one of them a tiny fertile crescent, a nucleus of life and a bulwark of civilization against the constantly encroaching desert. Little was known about these bygone cultures until the 20th century, until grave robbers and archaeologists began to discover significant clues.

One of the most astonishing discoveries was Sipán, where Moche nobles were buried between A.D. 200 and 600. The tombs first came to light in 1987, when Dr. Walter Alva, director of the nearby Brüning Museum, noticed the appearance of sophisticated artifacts on the local black market. Alva traced the items to Sipán, a hamlet in the sugarcane country east of the city of Chiclayo. The first tomb excavated by Alva's team was the richest ever found in Peru—a New World equivalent of King Tut's treasure: gold and silver ornaments, fabulous pottery, weapons, and weavings.

Exploring the site, I came across Luis Chero crawling on his hands and knees in the bottom of a six-foot pit. "This is the 12th tomb we have excavated at Sipán," he told me, brushing the dirt off his pants as he climbed out of the pit. As Sipán's chief archaeologist, Luis has been working the ruins for more than a decade, through searing summer heat, flash floods, and even an occasional riot. "After the first tomb was discovered, this place was invaded by people from the town. They divided up the area into claims and started digging. Police had to be called in, and they had to shoot in the air to disperse the grave robbers."

North of Chiclayo is another impressive archaeological site, the ruins of ancient Túcume. Standing next to the Pan American Highway, its 26 mud-brick pyramids cover more than 540 acres. Most were begun around A.D. 1100 by an offshoot group of the Moche. But Túcume may have been a place of religious pilgrimage for several thousand years before that. Many locals avoid the site, believing the ruins are haunted by ancient spirits. I shrugged off the legends, exploring the ruins alone in the fading light of a warm afternoon. Massive adobe walls towered over me as I ambled down a dusty path that had once been the city's main avenue. I stumbled onto the remains of a large reed boat, left behind by Norwegian adventurer Thor Heyerdahl of *Kon Tiki* fame. He began probing these ruins in the late 1980s, trying to find a cultural link between Túcume and the ancient South Pacific cultures.

Shamans, too, have long been attracted to Túcume, drawn by its magical powers. I found one of them living on the edge of the ruins, a short, stocky man named Victor Bravo. Like a desert fox, he had piercing eyes, black pools that never betrayed much about the man behind them. Bravo always seemed to be staring off into the distance, and I always caught myself looking around, wondering what he was glancing at—perhaps a spirit or demon invisible to mere mortals like myself.

"You just missed a virgin ceremony," Victor shot back when I asked if any shaman rites were pending. I wanted to ask if he had sacrificed the virgin in question, but Victor didn't look like the sort who would appreciate the humor. He did, however, let me in on a cermony late that day. He and his family had made makeshift, miniature hot-air balloons, with candles to provide heat for lift. Each balloon represented a plea or prayer, supplications to spirits both ancient and modern. Lighting the candles, the family cast the balloons aloft—a cortege of flickering lights drifting above the darkened pyramids.

Perhaps it was just coincidence, or maybe I'd vexed the evil spirits by treading on sacred ground at Túcume, but misfortune seemed to shadow me the next few days. Bandits attacked a bus on the Pan American only a few hours after I had driven the same stretch. A village bank was held up by robbers only a few hours after I had passed through. The third incident was the one that really sent a shiver up my spine: I spent a morning talking to fishermen at a tiny seaside hamlet called San José only to find out later that two of the men drowned in a boating accident that afternoon.

That was enough to get me moving again. I followed the Pan American down to the Chicama Valley, the heartland of *caballos de paso*, high-stepping horses that compete in dressage-like competitions. The breed has a colorful history. Early Spanish colonists taught their horses to walk in a peculiar manner—front legs curved outward, back legs driven against the ground—as a more effective way to travel across the coastal dunes. Over the centuries this practical skill evolved into one of Peru's most distinctive and beloved traditions.

"After 400 years of training, the high stepping is now passed down from generation to generation," Candy Moreno, a champion paso rider, explained to me at her family's *(Continued on page 138)*

FOLLOWING PAGES: *Colonial colonnades edge Lima's Plaza de Armas, recalling the era when this was the City of the Kings. Founded by conquistador Francisco Pizarro in 1535, the city became the showplace of Spanish South America.*

MAN AND BEAST *face off at the nation's oldest bullring—Plaza de Acho in Rímac, a Lima suburb. Backed by the towering bulk of Cerro San Cristóbal, the ring ranks among the top venues for the sport, attracting world-class matadors. Bullfighting remains an abiding passion for many Peruvians, who revel in its pomp and pageantry—and its inherent danger.*

OPPOSITE: *During the October Festival of Bullfighting for the Lord of the Miracles, thousands of spectators gather to critique the finesse of both human and bovine competitors.*

Fiddling for posterity, 65-year-old Amador Ballumbrosio hopes to pass along to his granddaughter the music he learned from his own grandfather. In his small community of El Carmen, near Pisco, most locals trace their ancestry to African slaves, brought here generations ago to work the area's cotton plantations.

Opposite: Young dancers take to the floor in the Ballumbrosio living room, as Amador's grandson drums out a beat that blends African and Peruvian rhythms.

Vasquez Hacienda. "Paso horses are very soft—you can ride them for eight hours and not get sore. And they are very steady. We have a contest for children. They carry a glass of water while riding a paso horse, and the winner is the one who spills the least." We watched as a trainer went round and round with a big chestnut stallion, patiently correcting a minor flaw in the front step. Another horse poked his head over the nearby fence, observing the scene with a somewhat patronizing sneer. "His name is Sol de Paijan," Candy said. "He was a grand paso champion. He's 28 years old, but we still use him as a stud."

I stumbled onto another Peruvian tradition a bit farther down the coast in the waterfront of Huanchaco. Here, fishermen still put to sea in boats woven from tortora reeds grown on a swampy plot north of town. The first time I ventured down to the beach was a sunny Sunday afternoon, but there wasn't a fisherman in sight. The waves had been taken over by surfers, teens from nearby Trujillo clad in wet suits and T-shirts. A couple of days later I went back at dawn. Just beyond the waves, half a dozen reed boats bobbed up and down in the swell as their masters trawled the waters offshore.

One by one the fishermen rode the waves in and landed on the beach, the sparse remnants of a reed-boat fishing fleet that once numbered in the hundreds. "We still make the boats ourselves," a middle-aged fisherman told me, his face weathered by years on the high seas. He described the process as not unlike weaving a large reed mat. "We usually alternate between two or three boats, because after a month on the water, they get very wet and very heavy." The locals only concession to modern times are styrofoam blocks stuffed into the bow to give the boats more buoyancy.

The fishermen were all nearing the age when it would no longer be practical to venture offshore. I asked if they would be the last generation of reed-boat fishermen. He scoffed at the notion and marched me down the beach, where a teenage fisherman was coming in. I helped the boy drag his waterlogged craft up the beach, surprised by its hefty weight. "I used to fish from the pier with a net," he told me. "But I saw what these guys were doing and decided to give it a try." He scooped up a basketful of shrimp and started toward the seafood restaurants that line the waterfront.

I drove the stretch of highway between Trujillo and Lima in a single day, grappling with relentless desert and thick coastal fog that dropped visibility to a couple of hundred feet. It was well after dark by the time Lima finally appeared, lights twinkling in the distance. Ready or not, I was about to confront the second largest city—after Los Angeles—on the Pacific coast of both Americas.

In truth, I wasn't looking forward to Lima—its celebrated pollution, poverty, traffic, and crime. There was also foul weather to contend with, the overcast skies that drape Lima for most of the year. That first morning I sat in my hotel room staring out the window at the pervasive gloom, wondering if I should press on into the desert again, leave this dreadful city behind after only a cursory glance. I eventually summoned the will to venture out into the streets.

Over the next few days, Lima slowly but surely enchanted me. Peru's capital is still plagued by mammoth problems. But I discovered that since the election of a new municipal government in 1996, the city has been improving. Legions of street sweepers comb the historic city center. Funds have gone into the restoration of ancient buildings. Police diligence has brought about a drastic plunge in pickpocketing and petty thievery. Civility is returning to Lima after years of bedlam.

Founded by conquistador Francisco Pizarro roughly 40 years after Christopher Columbus's first landfall in the Western Hemisphere, Lima has always been one of the grande dames of the Americas. Originally dubbed Ciudad de los Reyes (City of the Kings), Lima quickly grew into the most prosperous Spanish community in the New World, a place of Renaissance palaces and baroque churches that rivaled the grand cities of Europe. Lima was also an early center of learning, with the continent's oldest university (San Marcos, founded in 1551 and still in existence). But there is also a dark side to its past. For over two centuries, beginning about 1570, Lima was the South American bastion of the bloody Spanish Inquisition. Thousands of "heretics" were tortured and murdered inside the archbishop's palace and other religious strongholds, the corpses conveyed through underground passages to the catacombs beneath San Francisco Convent.

Lima continued to prosper until 1746, when a massive earthquake ravaged most of the old colonial center. The city didn't really blossom again until an early 20th-century economic boom sparked a new era of construction and population growth. Many of the magnificent buildings that grace the downtown area were constructed at that time, while outlying villages like San Isidro, Miraflores, and Barranco developed into stylish suburbs for Lima's upper class. In addition to its resident artists and music clubs, breezy seaside Barranco is a bastion of seviche, one of the culinary delights of Peru.

My first encounter with this marinated raw-fish dish was at Costa Verde, a restaurant that sprawls along Barranquito Beach, waves crashing against its plate glass windows. The dining room, as big as an airplane hangar, was flanked by buffet tables with almost 500 different items, ranging from lobster thermidor to vichyssoise. But it was the seviche, laced with fresh lime and a pinch of salt, that took my breath away. I became an instant fanatic. "There's a theory that seviche was slave food in ancient times," said Billy Hare, a Barranco artist who introduced me to some of the finer points of Peruvian cuisine. "Little pieces of seafood, scraps left over after the master had eaten. But there is another theory that the Inca may have eaten seviche, that it may have been a royal food."

At the southern extreme of Lima, *(Continued on page 147)*

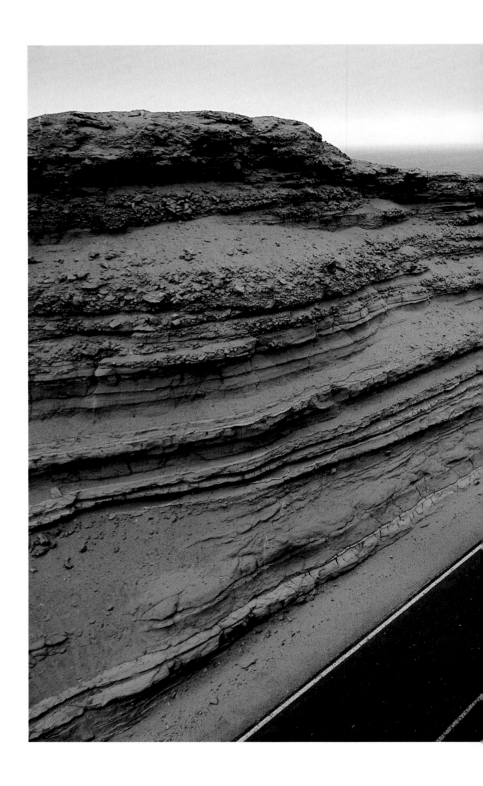

Lone truck pounds the Pan American between Nazca and Arequipa. Looping sinuously along the Pacific coast for hundreds of miles here, the highway has taken dozens of lives over the decades; ominous roadside crosses mark the spots where motorists have plunged to their demise.

Sᴀɴᴄᴛɪᴏɴᴇᴅ sᴘᴏʀᴛ: *Novices at Santa Catalina Monastery in Arequipa are encouraged to enjoy courtyard ball or a bit of group singing to ease their transition to the cloistered life. Founded in 1579 as a retreat for the daughters of wealthy colonial families, the convent now houses 30 nuns, aged 15 to 98.*

DESOLATE BEAUTY OF THE VALLE DE LA LUNA results from sculpting by wind and water over millennia. Among the world's driest deserts, parts of northern Chile's Atacama go for more than a century without recordable precipitation.

OPPOSITE: As if in supplication, fingers of a giant sculpted hand reach out of the relentless Atacama sands along the Pan American south of Antofagasta. Despite its desolateness, the Atacama abounds in geologic wonders: volcanoes, geysers, hot springs, even saline lakes where flamingos breed.

BEATIFIC BOY OF THE DESERT, *a young shepherd poses with his lamb. He and his family live in the wet, foggy stretch of northern Chile that surrounds the cloud forests of Fray Jorge National Park. Despite the dampness, cactus thrive here, and inventive villagers plant them in rows to form livestock pens.*

where shantytowns finally fade into pristine desert, rise the ruins of Pachacámac. Though the area was popular with pilgrims several centuries before the Inca came to power, they transformed Pachacámac into the most imposing spiritual complex along the entire Peruvian coast. Inveterate worshipers of the cosmos, the Inca constructed a number of remarkable adobe structures. The towering Temple of the Sun affords splendid views of sunsets even today. The sprawling ruins are enclosed within two arms of the Pan American Highway—the old two-lane road in the east and a swift new expressway in the west, which runs all the way down to Paracas.

In 1821 Gen. José de San Martín, who had already liberated his native Argentina and Chile from Spanish rule, waded ashore at Paracas and began his emancipation of Peru. With Simón Bolívar, the continent's other great liberator, pressing down from the north, Spanish resistance collapsed within three years. These days the sleepy port is more renowned as the gateway to Peru's premier coastal park, the wild and rugged Paracas National Reserve. Numerous creatures take refuge in its deep blue waters, including dolphins, whales, and giant leatherback turtles. Its lagoons and offshore rocks harbor millions of seabirds. Walking the salt flats along Paracas Bay, I watched as a shimmer of pink appeared on the water, a flock of flamingos taking flight over the bay.

An early morning earthquake woke me several days later and several hundred miles farther south in Nazca. Nothing major, mind you, but enough to give me a fright. Fields of rubble and ravaged buildings attest the fact that Nazca sits on the Peruvian equivalent of the San Andreas Fault. It has been repeatedly demolished by quakes. Yet tremors have never disturbed the enigmatic Nazca Lines on the northern edge of town, one of the enduring mysteries of the ancient world.

The Pan American Highway cuts a black swath across the plateau that harbors the prehistoric images created by these lines of stone. In fact, the road cleaves one entire figure (the "lizard")—not an act of indiscreet engineering, but because nobody knew the lines were here until 1929, when they were discovered during an aerial survey of Inca irrigation canals.

Paul Kosok and Maria Reiche were the first to study the lines. Reiche was mystically drawn to them and devoted the remainder of her life—50 odd years—to charting, sketching, and cleaning the stone effigies. There are more than two dozen in total, ranging from huge trapezoids to various zoomorphic forms that include a whale, a condor, a hummingbird, and llamas. There is also a bizarre humanoid image rendered on the flank of a rust-colored hill. Dubbed the "astronaut" by New Age gurus, the figure helped kindle the extraterrestrial theories hovering around the lines—that they function as carefully demarcated landing zones for spacecraft. But many other theories have been put forward as well to explain the purpose and origins of the lines. Some researchers feel that they have religious significance, while others claim they are some sort of ancient astronomical observatory related to overhead constellations. Most likely they were rendered by master artists of the Nazca culture, which flourished in this region from 100 B.C. to A.D. 700. But the riddle of their origins only adds to the allure of the place.

Reiche herself passed away just before I set off along the Pan American Highway, but I found her grave, still covered in fresh flowers and other tributes, beside her house in San Pedro. Her battered old Volkswagen van is parked out front, covered in her own hand-painted renderings of various lines; inside the house, her bedroom is very much as she left it, a simple bed, a cluttered drafting table, dozens of hand-drawn blueprints that detail the mysterious images.

The Pan American between Nazca and Arequipa is one of the most spectacular portions of the entire route. Creeping and crawling along precipitous cliffs that drop straight down to the sea, the highway here has taken more than its fair share of victims—as the many roadside crosses affirm. And every arroyo and ridge seems to have its own tale. North of Chala, the highway intersects the ancient Inca road that ran between Cuzco and the coast. Farther along, it dips into the lush Yauca Valley, filled with thousands of olive trees, progeny of the first olives carried to South America by the conquistadors. At Sacaco, it spans a wide stretch of shifting dunes, once the bottom of a prehistoric bay that Spanish archaeologist Roque Martin del Buey excavated shortly after World War II. The ten-million-year-old remains of a petrified whale he discovered is still there, as are most of the other bones he unearthed.

Another fossil of sorts is Santa Catalina Monastery in Arequipa, a day's drive south along the highway. Established in 1579 as a retreat for nuns from wealthy colonial families, the monastery was off-limits to the outside world until 1970, when the municipal government decreed that it must comply with local building codes. What the city inspectors found inside was astounding, a tiny city within a city with its own hospital, cemetery, and public baths. For all intents and purposes, life had changed little since the Middle Ages. Wooden fires stoked bake ovens, candles lit corridors at night, all washing was done by hand.

To fund newfangled things like electricity and plumbing, the nuns opened their doors to tourists on a limited scale. You still can't visit their private quarters, but other parts of Santa Catalina are part of a guided tour. "For a young woman to get admitted here, her family had to pay more than 2,000 silver coins and provide a dowry of 25 things that she could use during her life," Alexandra Revilla explained as we walked through the Courtyard of Silence, where novices spent their first year. "To leave the convent brought great shame to the family," Alexandra continued. "It was better to say you didn't have a daughter than to admit she had left."

The rest of Santa Catalina gradually unfolded before us, the most

Seaside Puerto Caliche, a restaurant in Antofagasta, offers a long view of Chile's Norte Grande—Great Northern—coast, including a massive wave-washed arch called La Portada.

Following pages: At a rodeo in the ranch country north of Santiago, Chilean cowboys compete together in teams, working against the clock to capture unruly steers. Traditional cowboy garb includes an Andalusian-style sombrero, poncho over a small jacket, and silver spurs that fit into perfectly carved wooden stirrups.

METHUSELAH OF THE DESERT, *the Chilean palm can live more than a thousand years. Once prevalent throughout Chile, the palms were decimated during the 19th century, felled for their sugar-sweet sap. These at the Oasis de la Campana escaped exploitation because the area was protected as a Jesuit-owned hacienda. Today, it serves as an ecological reserve safeguarding the now endangered tree.*

impressive colonial relic in all Peru. Various courtyards and plazas and dozens of pastel buildings are arranged along streets named after Spanish cities. Former cells around the cloisters contain original furnishings and artwork of past inhabitants; some are quite opulent, reflecting the fact that most of these women came from wealthy families. In fact, many cells are equipped with servant quarters, for the nuns rarely did their own cooking or cleaning. When I quipped about their cushy lifestyle, Alexandra had a quick comeback. "Yes," she said, "it was very comfortable. But you must remember, a nun had to stay here all her life."

Wandering down the Peruvian coast, I began to realize that size is everything in the desert. Perhaps it has something to do with survival of the fittest, but everything seems to take on immense proportions—pyramids, fossils, even convents—a pattern that continued even after I crossed into northern Chile. For in the heart of the Atacama Desert lies Chuquicamata, one of the world's largest open-pit copper mines and one of the few man-made things that can be seen from space. The statistics are phenomenal: 2.5 miles wide and 2,500 feet deep—yielding enough ore to produce 600,000 tons of refined copper annually.

"As you can imagine, it's a very big hole," said Patricio Huerta of the mine's public affairs department. But I wasn't prepared for just how big. I must have let out a gasp because Patricio laughed. I almost needed binoculars to see the dump trucks laboring in the bottom of the pit. Not ordinary dump trucks but gargantuan machines around a hundred times larger than the average family pickup. The hole is large enough to hold two Empire State Buildings stacked atop one another. And the digging isn't finished. "Over the next 25 years our goal is to go down about twice as deep," Patricio explained.

The Chuquicamata area was exploited for copper as early as the Inca period. But it was a pair of brothers from New York City—the Guggenheims of art-museum fame—who introduced the first modern mining techniques in 1911. Four years later they sold out to the Anaconda Company, which developed the site into a copper marvel. In 1971 President Salvador Allende nationalized the mine.

Copper may be king at present, but a hundred years ago a much different mineral ruled the Atacama—nitrate, or saltpeter—used in the manufacture of gunpowder and fertilizer. The nitrate boom began in the early 1870s and soon exploded into open warfare between Chile, Bolivia, and Peru, with the three countries jostling for the rich deposits. As part of the spoils of victory, Chile annexed the entire Atacama region from Bolivia, a wound that continues to fester between the two nations. By the early 20th century, the "nitrate kings," made rich off the backbreaking labor of thousands of miners toiling in the desert, were building fancy mansions in Santiago. The miners excavated the surface of dry lake beds with picks and shovels, extracting surface caliche that was then processed into nitrate crystals. Everything went bust just before World War I, when a formula for artificial nitrate was discovered in Europe. Now, nitrate ghost towns are scattered along the Pan American Highway between Iquique and Tal Tal. In places like Oficina Puelma, once home to 7,000 residents, only windswept adobe ruins remain. But near the town square a faded sign still proclaims "A Future in the Desert."

The Atacama's latest boom is tourism, although the numbers are still very small. Most visitors head for the tiny village of San Pedro de Atacama, tucked up into the little corner of northern Chile that borders Bolivia and Argentina. "The desert around here is just fantastic," said Rick Sinclair, my guide in the Atacama. "The light, the colors, the shapes. But I'll tell you the most amazing thing—the size, the sense of distance. Your mind can barely grasp the vastness of this place." A teaching job at one of the big copper mines near Antofagasta drew Rick and his wife from their native Australia in 1993. But it was the desert that made them stay long after that original contract had expired.

Rick is an Atacama addict with an uncanny knack for discovering gems in a seemingly empty wasteland. At sunset one day we ventured out to the aptly named Valle de la Luna. It was desert for sure, but all the colors of the rainbow were there in one form or another, garnishing the deeply chiseled canyons and cliffs that give the valley its otherworldly feel. Struggling up a hundred-foot sand dune, I was rewarded with a panorama of ash-capped volcanoes to the east and unrelenting desert to the west.

Next day Rick and I were up long before the sun appeared, driving through the dark on a dirt track that climbed into the Andes. We didn't see a single light, a solitary house, any sign of human habitation for nearly three hours. But the moon lit our way, casting shadows across the murky landscape. Above 12,000 feet I could feel the altitude: shortness of breath and a mild headache. Rick's 4x4 groaned, but we kept moving.

At the end of the road lay El Tatio, the world's highest geyser field. More than a hundred geysers populate a marshy valley in the shadow of three massive volcanoes. Only one of them explodes with anything like fury. But their combined presence was awesome, fumaroles that rose into corkscrews and mushroom clouds escaping into the early morning chill. It was bitterly cold, well below freezing. Rivulets around the geyser field were frozen solid. As the sun emerged, the geysers seemed to hiss with more fury, building up huge heads of steam, almost as if they were angry at the appearance of a rival heat source. I found myself wrapped in a geothermal fog, afraid I might accidentally step into one of the boiling pools. But the sun eventually won this battle of primal forces, as it does every day, and an hour after sunrise, the geysers fell into a gentle slumber.

Coming down from the mountains, Rick detoured to another of his favorite spots. Wedged into a fertile desert canyon was the village of Caspana, occupied since at least 800 B.C. and currently populated by the

Outmaneuvering rush hour gridlock, motorcycles rank as the vehicle of choice for many Santiago commuters. Chile's bustling capital and largest city thrives on manufacturing, finance, and trade.

Santiago's downtown coffee bars, like upscale Café Cousino, offer business-men a place to grab a bite—and even a quick kiss from a scantily clad waitress.

BYGONE ATMOSPHERE OF AGING ALLEYS *and jumbled rooflines characterizes Valparaíso's older neighborhoods. Victorian-era* ascensores *(funicular railways) still shuffle up and down the port city's notoriously steep hillsides.*

OPPOSITE: *Though high-rises ring its harbor and it ranks as Chile's busiest seaport, Valparaíso has never fully reclaimed the glory it enjoyed before 1914, when the opening of the Panama Canal redirected much of its business.*

descendants of the ancient Atacamano people. Caspana is about as post-card perfect as an Andean village can be: stone houses perched on red-rock cliffs, verdant terraces where farmers till the soil with bare hands, Indian women clad in gray bowler hats and colorful shawls. The retired farmer who looks after the village museum told me that, even after the Spanish built the church, the Indians never had much contact with them.

Several days later and nearly a thousand miles farther south along the Pan American, I found myself exploring a vastly different Chilean valley, the fertile rift that contains the national capital. After the long days of desert driving, it was something of a shock to confront a big city again. But Santiago is a most agreeable metropolis, an abode of parks, gardens, and riverside promenades. A city ripe for walking.

So walk I did. Through the Plaza de la Constitution and its famed Moneda Palace, surrounded by towering art deco buildings that give downtown Santiago the feel of 1930s Manhattan; along the leafy banks of the Río Mapoche, where I bought ice cream from an organ grinder; up Santa Lucia Hill with its mock fortress and artificial waterfalls; across vineyards of the Maipo Valley on the southern edge of the metropolitan area, where most of Chile's wine is produced; and through the rambling woods of the Parque Metropolitano, a vast open space in the heart of the city.

On the edge of the park, in Barrio Bellavista, I came upon a funky old house called La Chascona, where author Pablo Neruda spent much of his life. The design is a mélange of styles ranging from Spanish colonial to art deco, betraying Neruda's eclectic interests. His forte was poetry and history, yet Neruda was always a fiercely political person and a close friend of Salvador Allende. Several days after a military coup deposed Allende in 1973, Neruda died, some say from a broken heart.

Neruda was also a well-known eccentric, and La Chascona, one of three houses he built in Chile, is filled with his various collections—still life paintings, primitive sculptures, Russian dolls, maritime artifacts, thousands of books, and his Noble Prize for Literature (collected in 1971 when he was Chile's ambassador to France). "He was a ludicrous big boy who liked to play at making his own houses," Pablo Antunez of the Neruda Foundation said as we toured the property. One of the poet's eccentricities is in the dining room—a wooden cupboard with a secret door that leads into a pantry. During dinner parties he would go out the normal door and return several minutes later through the secret door—in disguise. "That's the boy in him," Pablo laughed. "Always playing tricks."

Leaving La Chascona, I took a nearby funicular to the top of San Cristobal, a 2,850-foot peak hovering above the city like a guardian angel. From its summit all of Santiago spread out before me. I lounged on a park bench, easily falling asleep in the warm afternoon sun. But my snooze was soon interrupted. A chilly breeze whipped in from the east, a reminder that high mountains weren't far away. The Andes were waiting.

IN THE SHADOW OF HUGE CARGO SHIPS, *a Valparaíso fisherman calmly paints his boat. The primary gateway for Chile's thriving export business, Valparaíso ships out megatons in copper, fruit, wine, and timber to ports worldwide.*

ARGENTINA

PHOTOGRAPHS BY SUSIE POST

F or almost a hundred years, Jesus has guarded La Cumbre Pass in the high Andes, a rugged snow-mantled landscape second only to the mighty Himalaya in height. His towering bronze statue—Cristo Redentor, Christ the Redeemer—was erected in 1904 to mark the end of a border dispute between Chile and Argentina. Nearly 30 years after the shrine was built, the Pan American Highway was chiseled through the remote pass, following an ancient llama and donkey route up and over the Andes. Today the serpentine road has to rank as one of the world's most thrilling mountain drives.

For more than half a century, this was the only way to drive from Santiago to Buenos Aires without detouring almost a thousand miles north or south. But the old road became obsolete almost overnight when the 4,500-foot-long Redentor Tunnel opened several thousand feet beneath the pass in 1980. The border checkpoint at La Cumbre eventually closed, and the high-mountain route was all but forgotten.

Nowadays, the only way to reach Cristo Redentor is from the Argentine side, along a rough gravel track that climbs almost vertically toward the clouds. The 13,000-foot pass is a bleak place devoid of vegetation and pounded by incessant wind. But it stares across a vast tableau of stone and ice wrapped in wispy clouds—the kind of vista that literally takes your breath away in a combination of altitude, vertigo, and admiration.

A hundred yards from the statue is the Chilean side, and I crossed the border to explore the ruins of an old stone hotel, the rooms packed with snowdrifts. Back on the Argentine side, I took refuge from the cold in a small café. The proprietor, an old-timer with a bushy mustache and skin nearly as parched as that of the mummies I'd seen in Peru, offered me hot coffee with a touch of cognac. Just the thing for the cold, he assured me. I asked him why you couldn't cross the border via La Cumbre Pass. "Because there's no longer a road," he laughed. "Back in 1978 we had a border conflict with Chile. Their army blew up the road with dynamite, so our guys couldn't get down there. They've never repaired it."

Beyond La Cumbre, the highway plunges steeply downward, hugging

GAUCHOS DRIVE PACK MULES *loaded with supplies for trekkers across the high desert foothills surrounding 22,835-foot Aconcagua, South America's highest peak. Once the cowboys of the Pampas, some gauchos have turned their skills to outfitting the hikers and climbers that brave the Andes backcountry.*

PRECEDING PAGES: *Strutting in a streetside tango, a couple dances to the beat of street musicians in Buenos Aires's port district, where the quintessentially Argentine dance got its start.*

RELAXING ATOP A TANKER loaded with water, volunteer firemen wait to ladle out libations to religious pilgrims walking the Pan American Highway in honor of the Virgin Mary.

PRECEDING PAGES: Taking on the Andes, an old stretch of the Pan American winds high up to La Cumbre Pass. In the 1980s a tunnel through the mountains below the pass made this section of the highway obsolete.

the banks of the Río de la Cuevas as it flows toward the Pampas more than a hundred miles distant. The highland scenery is starkly beautiful, a spectrum of blacks, browns, oranges, grays, and yellows created by the volcanism that continues to push the Andes higher and higher. Not far from the pass is Puente del Inca, a natural arch that leaps the river in one mighty bound. Beneath it, sulfur springs bubble forth from the bare stone and a grotto with statues of the Virgin Mary is frequented by climbers, who come to pray for good luck during their ascents of 22,835-foot Cerro Aconcagua, highest mountain in both the Western and Southern hemispheres. You can only see the peak from one point along the highway, the gravel parking lot in the area called Los Horcones. The huge white mountain is usually bathed in snow and ice, clouds encasing the summit.

The first community of any size beyond the mountains is Mendoza, a quintessential Argentine city. With bustling sidewalk cafés, sycamore-shaded avenues, and gracious plazas, Mendoza is a haven of European ambience in the otherwise barren land lying in the rain shadow of the Andes. Many of the residents descended from the Italians, Spaniards, Arabs, and central Europeans who flocked here after the railroad came in the late 19th century. The cultural mix accounts for the city's cosmopolitan flair, a certain savoir faire that's hard to match even in Buenos Aires.

Some 400 years old, Mendoza has witnessed a lot of history. In fact, it was from here in 1814 that Gen. José de San Martín recruited his vaunted Army of the Andes to launch an invasion of Chile. To honor his heroics, a section of the Pan American near Mendoza is named for him.

Mendoza sits at the heart of the Argentine wine industry, its surrounding countryside harboring more than 1,200 wineries—the single largest concentration in all Latin America. "What you find here are almost perfect conditions for growing grapes used in certain types of wine," said Claudia Zappala. She was showing me around the historic Bodega Giol, founded in 1896 by Italian immigrants. Mendoza's specialty is red wine: Cabernet Sauvignon, Merlot, and Malbec in particular. The main harvest occurs in February and March, culminating in the Fiesta de la Vendimia, when the city bubbles over with parades, balls, and libations.

Making a round of the Mendoza vineyards, I heard much the same story as in the Chilean wineries: One of the unexpected spin-offs of nouvelle democracy and a more open economy is a tremendous boom in grape production and wine exports. At the giant Concha y Toro operation, which operates vineyards in Mendoza and in Chile, I was told that their products were boycotted abroad until the late 1980s because of the political situation here. But now the business is growing very rapidly.

FACED WITH VAST DISTANCES and an empty heartland, many Argentine travelers take buses straight across the Pampas, marathon journeys that can last more than 24 hours. That seemed the best way to me as well to cover the 680 miles between Mendoza and Buenos Aires. I discovered these trans-Pampas, double-decker coaches are in many respects heirs to the old-time Pullman cars that once crossed the grasslands. The seats recline to almost horizontal and movies play from overhead monitors, as winsome young female attendants deliver drinks, meals, and pillows.

As we sped along the supersmooth highway, the scenery sweeping past my window faded from the vineyards and olive groves around Mendoza to the die-hard cattle country of San Luis and Córdoba provinces. The highway was a shimmering mirage, and the heat rising from the range-land created billowy white clouds against the endless, spring blue sky. I have no idea how many cows we may have passed—hundreds, maybe even thousands. When the sun finally slid behind the Andes, the terrain turned pitch-black with a darkness almost frightening in its immensity.

I awoke the next morning as the bus was just pulling up to a solitary roadside diner. While the other passengers dug into breakfast, I ambled out into the middle of the nearest pasture to watch the sunrise. Nestled in the grass lay bones, horns, and bits of cowhide. As far as I could see in every direction were grazing cattle, grass, and a few scattered trees.

Yet islands of civilization break this prairie sea—places like San Antonio de Areco, where I lingered for a couple of days. Founded in the early 18th century by Spanish missionaries, Areco is something of a shrine to gaucho culture, largely because of *Don Segundo Sombra*. The 1926 novel by local writer Ricardo Güiraldes romanticized the life and times of the Argentine cowboy in much the way Zane Grey's books idealized the individualism of the American West.

Despite a fine museum dedicated to the cowpoke legacy and workshops that still produce some of the finest leatherwork and silver in all Argentina, I didn't expect to find any bona fide gauchos in Areco. Except perhaps in the municipal cemetery, where both Ricardo Güiraldes and the real-life roll models for Don Segundo are buried. After all, nobody rounds up cattle with horses these days, not even in Argentina. Yet I stumbled onto a veritable herd of local cowboys doing what they do best these days—talking about the good old days over a couple of stiff drinks.

The gauchos were gathered at Bessonart *pulpería*, a two-story structure with a crumbling, white-plaster facade that doubles as a general store and saloon. The ground floor is one long room divided down the middle by an ancient wooden counter, patrons on one side, proprietor on the other.

FOLLOWING PAGES: One of South America's most revered shrines, the Basilica Nuestra Señora in Luján draws some four million pilgrims a year. Tradition holds that the basilica's famous statue of the Virgin chose this site for herself in 1630, when the oxcart pulling her from church to church bogged down here and wouldn't budge until the Virgin was removed.

DOWNED STEER AT ESTANCIA EL OMBU *casts a resigned eye skyward as three gauchos steady it during castration. Though estancias still fill the Pampas with grazing cattle, the old, romantic life in the saddle has given way to more mechanized ways of ranching.*

GATHERING PLACE FOR GAUCHOS, *Bessonart cantina in San Antonio de Areco serves as the symbolic center for Argentina's slowly dying cowboy culture.*

The gauchos started gathering around seven, a trickle at first and then a flood. Old men clad in berets and boots, red or black scarves tied around their necks, silver buckles supporting baggy pants, the trademark gaucho knife lodged in their waistbands. Many were bowlegged from so many years in the saddle. But they were quick with a smile, even for a stranger.

"The gauchos made our country," said Juan Camilo Echamendi, a cigarette perched beneath his thick gray mustache. "They fought the revolution, and they went everywhere, to every corner of Argentina, working with cattle. But now we stay in one place." Juan told me that the last cattle drive from Areco to the big stockyards near Buenos Aires, 70 miles to the east, had been 30 years ago. "It took about three days for five or six hombres to move 300 to 500 animals. At night we slept under the stars. We ate homemade cheese and bread and asado (barbecued meat). They don't do that anymore. Now they put the cattle in big trucks."

Juan introduced me to another of the patrons, a younger man clad in tight blue jeans and red beret, a glint of mischief in his eyes. His name was Manuel Güiraldes, one of Argentina's best polo players, grandnephew of the gaucho bard, and master of his great-uncle's historic La Porteña estancia on the outskirts of Areco. Much like his uncle Ricardo, Manuel was a natural entertainer, cracking jokes and whipping off short songs that kept the entire bar amused. It wasn't long before he invited me to spend a day on his spread.

Early the next morning I found myself staring down the avenue of huge leafy trees that leads to La Porteña. Built in the 1850s, it's one of the most splendid ranch houses in all Argentina, whitewashed walls and red-tile roof draped in bougainvillea and surrounded by lush gardens filled with parrots and other birds. Upstairs is the tranquil "writer's corner," where Ricardo Güiraldes penned his prose and poetry, including *Don Segundo*, published in 1927, a year before his death at the age of 42.

Coffee on the patio was followed by a ride across the estancia, almost 1,500 acres of grazing land and soybean fields along the banks of the Río Areco. Back at the home, I got a glimpse of the "polo room," where more than 50 trophies testified to my host's equestrian abilities. Then I played polo. Not on a real horse, but on a wooden pony that Manuel uses to practice his strokes. We ate lunch under a huge shade tree in the garden, washing down our beef asado with blood-red Mendoza wine. The afternoon seemed to linger forever, much like the surrounding Pampas.

Buenos Aires was only two hours east along the Pan American, but in attitude and atmosphere it might have been a century away. With nearly 13 million people, this is one of the great cities of the world, a metropolis that sprawls along the banks of the Río de la Plata and far onto the Pampas. No other South American capital so thoroughly dominates the political, economic, and cultural life of its country.

I could not have picked a more auspicious time to roll into town. It was the week of the International Tango Festival, the tumultuous end of another soccer season, and the 15th anniversary of the restoration of democracy. I settled into a regal belle epoque hotel (complete with wrought-iron elevator) near the Plaza San Martín.

Unlike other great cities, Buenos Aires doesn't have an outstanding landmark or edifice that embodies its image, no world-class museums or incredible ancient ruins. The attraction is life itself, the human theater that unfolds in the streets and plazas. Porteños, as the city's residents call themselves, rarely do anything without flair or emotion. Just getting coffee delivered to your place of work entails a formally clad waiter making his way through the downtown crowds, coffee swishing back and forth in an elegant ceramic cup perched on a silver platter. Ordering a simple steak becomes a three-act play, especially in *parrillas* (barbecued-meat restaurants) like the historic La Estancia. Here, a cavalier attitude toward the menu could result in six slabs of beef piled on a single plate.

"Everyone has their little secrets about preparing meat," said Tomas Pugliese, owner and master chef of a parrilla in the Recoleta district. "The way that you position the charcoal brickets or the wood. How long you let it cook. You can't do this in ten minutes. Meat must be barbecued for at least three hours before the meal, in a calm manner so that you don't burn it, so that you don't change the flavor. Argentines don't marinate, and we never eat with sauce or condiments. We want to taste the meat as it is."

Consuming copious portions of beef is one way Porteño men flaunt their machismo. They also scream at other drivers, whistle at women, and rampage through the streets when their favorite soccer team wins. Porteño women flaunt their femininity with short skirts, high heels, and exposed cleavage, strutting down sidewalks with the flair of supermodels working the catwalk. The genders come together in the tango, an art form that seems to reach deep into the Argentine soul. "The tango allows you to get very near a woman, and this is a very special thing," Oscar Velazquez, a well-known tango dancer, told me. But the obsession goes beyond sensuality. Tango embodies two aspects of the Argentine character: a nostalgia for the past and a slowly growing optimism about the present and future.

Over drinks in a sidewalk café, Oscar and I discussed the history of the tango. Although its origins are somewhat murky, the dance was born around 1860 in the poorer barrios of Buenos Aires, where the descendants of black slaves lived side by side with recent Italian and Spanish immigrants. Considered vulgar by the city's "old money" residents, the dance was confined at first to lowly barrios and bordellos. But as the city's immigrant population exploded at the end of the 19th century, the tango became a nationwide phenomenon, as much a symbol of Argentina as the gaucho or the T-bone steak.

Now more than a century old, the tango is experiencing a widespread revival among Porteños, especially *(Continued on page 182)*

Swaying to a sultry tango beat, dancers fill the floor at the Club Alegro, among the many Buenos Aires nightspots that start to throb with music and motion after midnight. In recent years, Argentina's younger generation has rediscovered the century-old dance, turning it into the latest fashion.

FOLLOWING PAGES: Perhaps the world's widest street, Avenida 9 de Julio cuts a wide swath through downtown Buenos Aires. With 33 million people— 40 percent of the country's population—Argentina's capital prides itself on beautiful women, flashy soccer players, and thick steaks.

GHOSTS OF ARGENTINA'S DISAPPEARED *haunt the Plaza de Mayo in Buenos Aires, their shapes and names drawn on the stones as reminders of the former military junta's inhumanities. During the junta's "dirty war," waged from 1975 to 1982, thousands of antijunta activists were taken captive and never seen again.*

OPPOSITE: *White-scarved Madres de Plaza de Mayo gather every Thursday, mourning the loss of loved ones who disappeared during the former regime and imploring the current government for information on their fate.*

179

ROBED AND CROWNED ESTATUA VIVIENTE (*street performer Javier Alejandro Lewin*) *adds her/his own panache to the rambunctious atmosphere on pedestrians-only Florida Street, where luxury stores, acrobats, and street messiahs all compete for the attention of passersby.*

the young. They view the music, lyrics, and dance as allegorical links to a more innocent era, before the country was ruled by ruthless generals. "The tango reflects what's happening in Argentina," Oscar told me. "Ten years ago it was just a dance for people like me. But now the tango is alive again, a symbol of the new Argentina."

The resurrection was obvious during the International Tango Festival, and at every concert or dance exhibition I attended, teenagers and college students were always the first to rise with standing ovations. Although the older stars—like the legendary Quintet Real—are still in the vanguard, a new generation of singers and musicians is taking the stage, adhering to the tango's roots while introducing new elements borrowed from such diverse forms as samba, blues, and folk music.

Despite its dancing-in-the-streets atmosphere, Buenos Aires is also imbued with a slightly melancholy air, a grim subtext underlying its new hopefulness. From 1975 to 1982, Argentina was ruled by a military dictatorship that waged a "dirty war" against its own people. Thousands of intellectuals, journalists, and political dissidents disappeared. A full accounting of the regime's epidemic torture and murder has never been compiled.

The generals tried to distract public opinion from their atrocities by invading the British-held Malvinas (Falkland) Islands in 1982, but that military debacle ultimately led to the junta's downfall. There is no small irony in the fact that the Malvinas Memorial to those who died in the Falklands faces the Torre de los Ingleses, a Big Ben look-alike that long symbolized the enduring friendship between Argentina and Great Britain.

There is a conspicuous absence of any memorial to the thousands of "disappeared" who perished during the dirty war. But that doesn't mean the victims have been forgotten. The mothers of the disappeared were out in force during my week in Buenos Aires, parading through Plaza de Mayo, demanding a full accounting of all those who were kidnapped and killed by the former regime. Clad in their trademark white scarves, carrying photos of abducted family members, they went round and round the plaza, their eyes on Casa Rosada, the pink presidential palace that squats at one end of the square. "This is for the mothers and grandmothers all over the country who are still wondering where their loved ones have gone," said one of the demonstrators. "It's still an open wound," said another.

SOUTH OF BUENOS AIRES, the Pan American Highway passes broad stretches of prairie and farmland—maize, wheat, soybeans, potatoes—interrupted only by scattered urban outposts. The highway touches the sea at Bahía Blanca. A few miles farther south, at a woebegone place called Pedro Luro, it crosses the Río Colorado into Patagonia.

Much like Siberia or the Sahara, just the name Patagonia is enough to conjure images of a vast, unfettered wilderness, a place beyond the pale of civilization. It was the explorers sailing with Ferdinand Magellan for the Spanish crown who came up with the name. In 1520 they made the first European landfall in what is now Argentina. On seeing the local Indians, they dubbed them *patagoni*, big feet, probably because of their tall height and guanaco moccasins. After that, the Spanish essentially ignored the region, writing it off as untenable for colonial occupation. Not until centuries later did the Argentines finally get around to settling their savage southern frontier. Even then it was mostly foreigners, especially the Welsh, who undertook much of the pioneer push. Patagonia remains largely empty, the realm of sheep farms, windswept beaches, and snowy mountains that seem to stretch forever.

The monotony of the Patagonian coast is broken by an enormous anvil-shaped headland called the Peninsula Valdés, which juts out into the South Atlantic. Renting a car in Puerto Madryn, I drove a dusk-to-dawn circuit of the gravel roads that crisscross the peninsula. At first glance, the entire area seemed a wasteland. But closer inspection revealed an overwhelming wealth of wildlife, a Patagonian version of the Serengeti Plain.

Peering over the edge of a steep cliff near Punta Delgada, I spied thousands of elephant seals and southern sea lions on the beach below, basking in the sun, splashing through the surf, protecting their turf with loud, aggressive deportment. On the northern shore of Caleta Valdés lagoon, I stumbled onto flocks of rhea, large flightless birds related to the ostrich; and herds of guanaco, rust-colored cameloids. At Punta Norte I spotted another large sea lion colony, as well as a pesky armadillo, and a family of gray fox that had made their homes around the ranger station.

But the highlight of the day was whale watching. At the sleepy beachside town of Puerto Pirámides, I crawled into a small wooden boat with half a dozen other people from Holland, Spain, and Switzerland. Local wildlife guide Mariano de Franceschi cranked the outboard engine to life and steered us toward the southern flank of the peninsula, a breeding ground for right whales.

It wasn't long before Mariano spotted a couple of behemoths, a mother and newborn grazing in shallow water. He maneuvered the boat right beside them, close enough to reach out and scratch their backs—although Mariano was quick to point out that touching the whales was forbidden. "About 20 percent of the world's right whale population comes into the Golfo Nuevo to breed each year," Mariano related. "That's 400 to 700 animals, depending on the year. The big ones, they can weigh between 25 and

FOLLOWING PAGES: Established by Italian immigrants in the 19th century, La Boca—a neighborhood at the edge of modern-day Buenos Aires—remains fiercely proud of its no-frills alleyways and corrugated-metal homes. In recent years, artists, musicians, artisans, and tourists have also discovered the dilapidated charms of this waterfront district.

TANGO TERRITORY, *Buenos Aires's Señor Tango dinner club pulls in a fast and furious crowd most nights. To Argentines, dancing is only part of the tango's appeal. A song's melody and lyrics add their own magic to the mix.*

45 tons." I asked Mariano how they got their name. "Because they were the right whale for hunting," he answered. "The correct whale. They swim very slowly, they spend a long time on the surface, and they give a lot of oil and meat." Like many marine species, right whales had been hunted to the verge of extinction by the early 20th century. Peninsula Valdés is one of the few places where the population has not declined.

Among Patagonia's human denizens are the descendants of Welsh immigrants who settled the Chubut Valley during the latter half of the 19th century. Driven from their native Wales by poverty and political disagreements with their English overlords, the Welsh established towns like Trelew, Rawson, and Dolavon along the banks of the Río Chubut. Most had been coal miners back home, but in Patagonia they were forced to live off the land as farmers, fishermen, and herders. Within several decades they transformed what had been a desert wasteland into an agricultural oasis of wheat fields, fruit orchards, and verdant pastures.

One of the more remarkable things about the Patagonian Welsh is the degree to which they have remained Gaelic despite their fusion into modern Argentine society. On a bright blue Sunday morning in Trelew, I slipped into the Capilla Tabernacle, a stout brick church erected in 1889. About 50 people were already crammed into the wooden pews; half of them were children, many with blond hair and blue eyes and no doubt the Welsh surnames—Lewis, Jones, Davis—that still predominate in this valley. The readings from the Bible were in Spanish. But the hymns that punctuated each missive were unabridged Welsh. Their slow-rolling tempo somehow matched the mood of both the long-lost homeland in the British Isles and the new home at the southern extremity of the Americas.

"I think every day we're becoming more Welsh than Wales itself," said 75-year-old Marta Rees, owner of the Plas y Coed teahouse, that quintessentially Gaelic institution. Hers is located in Gaiman, the most solidly Welsh of all the Chubut towns. "Before only the old people spoke Welsh. But over the last ten years it's become more popular among the young people." Marta traces the revival to the early 1970s, when a large celebration was held to mark a century of Welsh immigration. The festivities revived ties with Mother Wales and were the beginning of a regular exchange of students and Welsh-language teachers.

"This was the first teahouse in Gaiman," Marta said proudly of the Plas y Coed, founded in the 1940s. "The whole thing was my mother-in-law's idea. In the beginning it was more for her friends who came around to drink tea, but then she made it an official business." And a serious one. Marta's Welsh teas feature irresistible carrot cake, apricot sponge cake, frozen raspberry-and-cream pie, homemade berry jams, and biscuits with melted cheese made from the milk of Chubut cows.

I carried my leftovers onto the bus that night. Another 830 miles of desert and prairie, broken only by *(Continued on page 192)*

WIDE SMILE FOR WELSH TEA *at the Plas y Coed teahouse in the Patagonian town of Gaiman. Welsh settlers have occupied the Chubut Valley here in southern Argentina since the mid-19th century. Recent interest in roots has resurrected the Welsh language, its songs, and teatime traditions.*

LOBOS MARINOS—SEA LIONS—*loll on a beach rimming Penînsula Valdés, a dramatic headland along Patagonia's Atlantic coast. Bulls, cows, and calves often collect on this stretch of sand at high tide, the males barking and posturing at each other with mock-machismo threats.*

sporadic habitations, still lay between me and the Pan American Highway's endpoint, at the southern tip of the South American mainland. My final destination was Río Gallegos, the southernmost city on the Argentine mainland and the jumping-off point for many of the natural attractions of southern Patagonia. Even on the verge of summer, it was a cold place in both temperature and spirit. Few of the Gallegans looked especially happy, despite the wealth that has poured in from nearby oil fields.

A couple of hours east of Río Gallegos lies one of Argentina's greatest natural assets, Moreno Glacier. The 22-mile-long tongue of ice spills through a massive gap in the Andes and down into the aquamarine waters of Lago Argentino. The spectacle leaves you speechless, not just the frozen giant but the snowy peaks, the dense forests, and the most pristine sky imaginable. Many people liken the glacier's facade to an ice castle, but for me the wildest thing was its color: cotton candy blue. Something you wanted to reach out and touch…if it weren't so dangerous. Since 1988 the Argentine park service has limited direct access to the glacier's facade, but in the two decades prior to that 32 people were killed by falling ice. "When a big chunk of ice hits a rock, it explodes like glass," Ranger Gretel Müller explained. "When it hits the water, it can cause a tidal wave on the lake."

On my very last day at the southern end of the Pan American, I drove south from Río Gallegos, beyond the point where the pavement finally peters out into a rough gravel road. Following the signs, I headed to Cabo Virgenes, the southernmost point on the Argentine mainland. I drove until there was no road left. Then I walked, down to the beach at the tip of the cape where a colony of Magellanic penguins make their home.

At first I was disappointed—no more than a couple of hundred birds where there were supposed to be thousands. I watched them for a while and got ready to leave. Rather than walk straight back to the car, I detoured along a nature trail through a scrub-filled valley behind the beach. Almost at once a curious sound arose from the vegetation: a dissonance of birds, thousands of them. Under every plant a burrowed nest held one or two chicks. The sandy lanes between were like penguin highways, black-and-white heads bobbing between bushes and beach.

This was finally the end of the road, a journey that had kicked off months before on the banks of the Rio Grande. But somehow it was very much like the beginning. Marching in single file across the valley, the penguins were almost a mirror image of the shoppers I had seen crossing the bridge between Mexico and the U.S. Standing at the southern tip of the Americas, I thought about all the other people I'd met along the highway—coffee pickers and tango dancers, matadors and gauchos, fishermen and fashion photographers, a compendium of modern Latin American society, everyone going about their own business yet indelibly linked by a ribbon of asphalt called the Pan American Highway. It had indeed been a long road south. But worth every mile.

SOLE INHABITANTS OF THE CONTINENT's *southernmost tip, a colony of some 30,000 Magellanic penguins call Cabo Virgenes home. Preferring warmer climes, this species is found farther north than its more cold-loving, Antarctic compatriots.*

FOLLOWING PAGES: *Centerpiece of Los Glaciares National Park, 22-mile-long Moreno Glacier spills out of the Chilean Andes and into Patagonia's Lago Argentino. The enormous chunks of ice it calves can send tidal waves crescendoing across the lakefront.*

Long Road South: The Pan American Highway

By Joseph R. Yogerst

Photographs by Susie Post and Melissa Farlow

Published by the National Geographic Society

John M. Fahey, Jr.　*President and Chief Executive Officer*

Gilbert M. Grosvenor　*Chairman of the Board*

Nina D. Hoffman　*Senior Vice President*

Prepared by the Book Division

William R. Gray　*Vice President and Director*

Charles Kogod　*Assistant Director*

Barbara A. Payne　*Editorial Director and Managing Editor*

David Griffin　*Design Director*

Staff for this book

John Agnone　*Project Editor and Illustrations Editor*

K. M. Kostyal　*Text Editor*

Cinda Rose　*Art Director*

Mary E. Jennings　*Researcher*

Carl Mehler　*Director of Maps*

Joseph F. Ochlak　*Map Researcher*

Michelle H. Picard　*Map Production*

Gregory Ugiansky

Martin S. Walz

R. Gary Colbert　*Production Director*

Richard Wain　*Production Project Manager*

Lewis R. Bassford　*Production Manager*

Janet A. Dustin　*Illustrations Assistant*

Peggy Candore　*Assistant to the Director*

Kevin G. Craig　*Staff Assistants*

Dale-Marie Herring

Deborah Patton　*Indexer*

Manufacturing and Quality Control

George V. White　*Director*

John T. Dunn　*Associate Director*

Vincent P. Ryan　*Manager*

Phillip L. Schlosser　*Financial Analyst*

The world's largest nonprofit scientific and educational organization, the National Geographic Society was founded in 1888 "for the increase and diffusion of geographic knowledge." Since then it has supported scientific exploration and spread information to its more than nine million members worldwide.

The National Geographic Society educates and inspires millions every day through magazines, books, television programs, videos, maps and atlases, research grants, the National Geography Bee, teacher workshops, and innovative classroom materials.

The Society is supported through membership dues and income from the sale of its educational products. Members receive NATIONAL GEOGRAPHIC magazine—the Society's official journal—discounts on Society products, and other benefits.

For more information about the National Geographic Society and its educational programs and publications, please call 1-800-NGS-LINE (647-5463), or write to the following address:

National Geographic Society
1145 17th Street N.W.
Washington, D.C. 20036-4688 U.S.A.

Visit the Society's Web site at
www.nationalgeographic.com.

Library of Congress Cataloging-in-Publication Data

Yogerst, Joseph R.
　　Long road south : the Pan American Highway / Joseph R. Yogerst.
　　　p. cm.
　　Includes index.
　　ISBN 0-7922-7845-3 -- ISBN 0-7922-7844-5
　　　1. Pan American Highway System. 2. Latin America--Description and travel. I.
National Geographic Society (U.S.) II. Title.

　HE358.Y63 1999
　918.04'39

99-049566

Composition for this book by the National
Geographic Society Book Division. Printed
and bound by R.R. Donnelley & Sons, Willard,
Ohio. Color separations by NEC, Nashville,
TN. Dust jacket printed by Miken Inc.
Cheektowaga, N.Y.

INDEX

NOTES ON THE CONTRIBUTORS

California-based JOSEPH R. YOGERST has written for numerous international publications, including the *Washington Post, Los Angeles Times,* and *Condé Nast Traveler.* He is a three-time winner of the Society of American Travel Writers' Lowell Thomas Award. His *Vietnam: Land of Nine Dragons,* won the Best Travel Book of 1992. He is currently at work on an upcoming National Geographic publication on national parks of the world.

SUSIE POST has been a freelance photojournalist since 1990. Her passion for documenting people's lives has led her to both magazine work and work with development organizations. Her most recent article in the NATIONAL GEOGRAPHIC featured life along the New River in the eastern U.S. She has served on the faculty of the Missouri Photo Workshop and is currently professional-in-residence at Western Kentucky University.

MELISSA FARLOW's work has ranged from covering American national parks in NATIONAL GEOGRAPHIC to small-town life in the Midwest to family life in sub-Saharan Africa. She has won awards in the National Press Photographers' Association annual Pictures of the Year competition and is a faculty member of the Missouri Photo Workshop.

ACKNOWLEDGMENTS

The Book Division and the writer and photographers of this book would like to thank the following people: Ibeth Acuna, Julie Ang, Claudio Adriasola, Marcelo Asis, Paige Bierma, Mariano Boj, Allen Boraiko, Milagros Bonifaz, Nancy Chappell, Carolina Chia, Alicia Ciarimboli, José Esteves, Rosalba Farfan, Nancy Felix, Alberto Garay Pillco, Rosalie Guerrero, Billy Hare, Santiago Harker, Mark Johnson, Cecilia Larrabure, Victoria Milán, Maribeth Mellin, Mayu Mohan, Silvina Ojeda de Cvitanich, Rose and Eddie Post, Adam Rust, Juan Sabaneta, Miguel Salguero, Marissa Silvera, Rick Sinclair, Percy Tapia, José Viquez, David Wroughton, and Mauricio Yonfa. In addition, we thank Joyce M. Caldwell for her careful reading of the final manuscript.

ADDITIONAL READING

The reader may wish to consult the *National Geographic Index* for related articles and books. The following sources may also be of interest: Raymond F. and Audrey Pritchard, *Driving the Pan-American Highway to Mexico and Central America;* Linda Schele, *The Blood of Kings: Dynasty and Ritual in Maya Art;* and the Library of Congress Country Studies/Area Handbooks for Central and South America. In addition, the following travel-guide series to Central and South America offer insights into history, culture, and travel logistics: Handbook Guides (Moon Publications); Lonely Planet Shoestring Guides; and Rough Guides.